C000127855

Dilemmas and Decision Making in Midwifery

Other books you may be interested in:

Academic Writing and Referencing for your Nursing Degree
Jane Bottomley and Steven Pryjmachuk   ISBN 978-1-911106-95-1

Communication Skills for your Nursing Degree
Jane Bottomley and Steven Pryjmachuk   ISBN 978-1-912096-65-7

Critical Thinking Skills for your Nursing Degree
Jane Bottomley and Steven Pryjmachuk   ISBN 978-1-912096-69-5

Learning Disability Nursing
Ruth Northway and Paula Hopes   ISBN 978-1-914171-35-2

Psychopharmacology, Second Edition
Herbert Mwebe   ISBN 978-1-914171-44-4

Studying for your Nursing Degree
Jane Bottomley and Steven Pryjmachuk   ISBN 978-1-911106-91-3

To order our books please go to our website www.criticalpublishing.com or contact our distributor Ingram Publisher Services, telephone 01752 202301 or email IPSUK.orders@ingramcontent.com. Details of bulk order discounts can be found at www.criticalpublishing.com/delivery-information.

Our titles are also available in electronic format: for individual use via our website and for libraries and other institutions from all the major ebook platforms.

Dilemmas and Decision Making in Midwifery

A practice-based approach

Edited by
Kenda Crozier
and Julia Hubbard

First published in 2023 by Critical Publishing Ltd

All rights reserved. No part of this publication may be reproduced, stored in a retrieval system, or transmitted in any form or by any means, electronic, mechanical, photocopying, recording or otherwise, without prior permission in writing from the publisher.

The authors have made every effort to ensure the accuracy of information contained in this publication, but assume no responsibility for any errors, inaccuracies, inconsistencies and omissions. Likewise, every effort has been made to contact copyright holders. If any copyright material has been reproduced unwittingly and without permission the Publisher will gladly receive information enabling them to rectify any error or omission in subsequent editions.

Copyright © 2023 Juliet Albert, Melanie Applegate, Kylie Burke, Ella Caine, Kenda Crozier, Kelda Folliard, Nicky Hadlett, Julia Hubbard, Jo Knox, Katherine Letley, Helen Meehan, Jayne Needham, Kirstin Pope, Ruth Sanders, Georgina Sosa, Jemma Thorne and Kirsty Tweedie

British Library Cataloguing in Publication Data
A CIP record for this book is available from the British Library

ISBN: 978-1-915080-23-3

This book is also available in the following e-book formats:
EPUB ISBN: 978-1-915080-24-0
Adobe e-book ISBN: 978-1-915080-25-7

The rights of Juliet Albert, Melanie Applegate, Kylie Burke, Ella Caine, Kenda Crozier, Kelda Folliard, Nicky Hadlett, Julia Hubbard, Jo Knox, Katherine Letley, Helen Meehan, Jayne Needham, Kirstin Pope, Ruth Sanders, Georgina Sosa, Jemma Thorne and Kirsty Tweedie to be identified as the Authors of this work have been asserted by them in accordance with the Copyright, Design and Patents Act 1988.

Text and cover design by Out of House Limited
Project management by Newgen Publishing UK
Printed and bound in Great Britain by 4edge, Essex

Critical Publishing
3 Connaught Road
St Albans
AL3 5RX

Printed on FSC
accredited paper

www.criticalpublishing.com

Contents

Meet the editors

Kenda Crozier is Professor of Midwifery and Dean of the School of Health Sciences at the University of East Anglia, UK. She is registered with the NMC as a nurse and midwife. Kenda was awarded a PhD from the University of Ulster in 2005; her research and teaching interests include midwifery models of care related to vulnerable groups, technology use in maternity and women's mental health and well-being. She has developed curricula in nursing, midwifery and advanced practice nationally and internationally. In 2022, she led a national programme to develop a capability framework and education and career pathway for advanced practice in midwifery in collaboration with Health Education England. She is visiting Professor at the University of Sharjah in the United Arab Emirates and Boronomajani College of Nursing in ChiangMai, Thailand.

Julia Hubbard is Professor of Clinical Health Education at the University of East Anglia. She is an experienced academic, having worked in university-level healthcare education since 1993. During that time, she has been involved in curriculum development and course delivery across a range of healthcare professions at undergraduate and postgraduate levels, both nationally and internationally. Her current role as innovation lead for the School of Health Sciences involves seeking new education opportunities to meet the changing healthcare needs of the UK population.

Meet the contributors

Juliet Albert is a qualified midwife who opened the Acton African Well Woman Centre at Queen Charlotte's and Chelsea Hospital in 2008. The clinic pioneered an innovative holistic model of care, winning a Guardian Public Service Award in 2011. It is now known as the Sunflower Clinic. Juliet has contributed to projects with the Department of Health and Barnardo's to prevent female genital mutilation (FGM) and raise awareness. Currently maternity FGM lead at Imperial College Healthcare NHS Trust, she has provided training to countless midwives, doctors and other frontline professionals. Her involvement in Somali women's networks and teaching contributes to raising awareness in communities about the law and dangers of FGM to women and girls. Juliet has a Masters in advanced practice midwifery from Kings College, University of London and has co-authored the RCM's FGM online package. She is an RCM Fellow and is currently undertaking a NIHR-funded PhD at the University of Nottingham.

Melanie Applegate is a midwifery clinical educator and research assistant at the University of East Anglia. She is registered with the NMC and has interests in the culture within midwifery and the perception of midwifery within society. She has coordinated projects leading to the development of a national education and career capability framework for advanced practice in midwifery.

Kylie Burke is a part-time lecturer in midwifery at the University of East Anglia, where she has worked since 2021. She has a MSc in midwifery and is registered as a nurse (adult) and midwife with the NMC and continues to work part time as a delivery suite midwife in the NHS. Her teaching interests include emergency midwifery management, simulation-based learning and care for vulnerable women in maternity services.

Ella Caine has been a registered midwife since 2000. She is a midwifery lecturer at the University of East Anglia and works clinically and as a professional midwifery advocate at the Norfolk and Norwich University Hospital. During her career she has worked in a variety of other roles including co-teaching obstetric emergency management in Spain and South America and providing expert midwifery reports for the court in clinical negligence cases. She is an editorial board member of *The Practising Midwife*. Currently she is a Darzi Fellow in south-west London working on a challenge to improve maternal health inequalities for minoritised women and birthing people.

Kelda Folliard is a clinical academic midwife. She is a midwifery lecturer at the University of East Anglia and specialist midwife for perinatal mental health and complex social factors at Norfolk and Norwich University Hospital. Kelda's teaching and research interests include perinatal mental health and the psychology of childbearing. Her doctoral research examines the lived experience of perinatal anxiety. Kelda is a midwifery ambassador for the national Transforming Perceptions of Midwifery programme.

Nicky Hadlett is a midwifery lecturer at the University of East Anglia. She worked as a midwife in the UK and overseas before moving into higher education. She has a wealth of experience as midwifery programme lead supporting students and clinical assessors in the clinical learning environment, as well as leading curriculum development, implementation and evaluation. With over 25 years' experience in university healthcare education, she is now Quality Lead for her university school and has external involvement in curriculum quality monitoring.

Jo Knox is a midwifery lecturer and previously was clinical educator at the University of East Anglia and registered with the NMC as a nurse and a midwife. Jo achieved a MSc in midwifery in 2011 and has worked across all areas of midwifery, including working as a specialist fetal surveillance midwife. Jo is a qualified midwifery newborn and infant physical examination practitioner. She has worked on regional quality improvement projects in the east of England and her interests lie in physiological birth, emergency care and quality improvement.

Katherine Letley is a midwifery lecturer at the University of East Anglia with a Masters in international development. She is currently studying part time for her PhD at City, University of London, examining the relationship between midwives and Syrian refugee women. Katherine also works as the maternity consultant for City of Sanctuary UK and co-ordinates their national project to develop available services for people seeking sanctuary in pregnancy and early parenthood.

Helen Meehan is a lecturer in health sciences at the University of East Anglia and an NMC registered nurse and midwife. Teaching across the undergraduate and post-registration programmes, she has an interest in leadership and quality issues. She has been a reviewer with the Commission for Health Improvement, the Quality Assurance Agency and Healthcare Inspectorate Wales. Helen has worked with the NMC as a reviewer of Local Supervisory Authorities and a 'fitness-to-practise' panelist. She was a supervisor of midwives and supports her colleagues at the Queen Elizabeth Hospital King's Lynn NHS Foundation Trust as a professional midwifery advocate.

Jayne Needham is lead midwife for education at the University of East Anglia. She trained as a nurse, working in intensive care before becoming a midwife. Jayne has a special interest in high-dependency care, and this is the subject of her ongoing doctoral research. She leads on the international opportunities for midwifery students at the University of East Anglia and has links with the Institute of Nursing Sciences in Belgaum, India, through a funded project to support development of emergency training in midwifery.

Kirstin Pope is a midwifery clinical educator at the University of East Anglia, where she is evaluated highly by learners for her contributions to simulation learning activities and support for student midwives in the practice learning environment. She is registered with the NMC and is an experienced midwife. She has worked across all areas within midwifery when working clinically and her passion lies with postnatal care.

Ruth Sanders is a midwifery lecturer at the University of East Anglia, currently undertaking a professional doctorate in health and social care. She is a member of the Royal College of Midwives Editorial Board and an Ambassador for Cavell Nurses Trust. Her research and teaching interests include decision making and health communication, pain management, health humanities and reflective practice. She has been involved in the development of frameworks for advanced clinical practice in midwifery nationally. She is a visiting tutor for King's College London and enjoys writing for a range of midwifery journals.

Georgina Sosa has been a midwife for 27 years, having trained and worked at the Whittington Hospital in London where her passion to support women and educate health professionals regarding female genital mutilation (FGM) commenced. Georgina moved to Norfolk and worked as a clinical midwife, clinical manager and governance midwife, and completed a PhD exploring midwifery one-to-one support in labour within midwife-led birth environments. Her research has been presented internationally and published in academic journals. Georgina has worked in all areas of midwifery, but she has a particular passion for enhancing physiological processes in labour and caring for women and training professionals regarding FGM. In 2017, her passion for teaching led her to academia at the University of East Anglia. Since 2021, Georgina has been working as an assistant professor at Fatima College of Health Sciences in Abu Dhabi, where she co-developed the only mid-wifery BSc programme in the United Arab Emirates.

Jemma Thorne is a clinical educator at the University of East Anglia. She is an experienced midwife and still works as a bank midwife for the Norfolk and Norwich University Hospital. During her time as a midwife, she has worked as a core member in midwifery-led birthing units and as a community midwife. Her passion lies in supporting physiological birth.

Kirsty Tweedie is course director for the BSc in Midwifery at the University of East Anglia. She is a registered midwife and neonatal examiner with a background as a delivery suite lead. She has experience of working in the UK and in Cyprus. Kirsty has been involved in midwifery education for ten years. She teaches pre-registration midwifery, medical and paramedic science students, and is the lead for the provision of the neonatal and infant physical examination module which is delivered at MSc level. She has developed curricula for midwifery and is recognised nationally for her work in collaborative learning in practice, a model of coaching for learners in practice.

Introduction

Kenda Crozier and Julia Hubbard

Midwifery is a profession distinct from nursing and other professions allied to medicine. Midwives' scope of practice centres on the reproductive health of women throughout pregnancy, childbirth and the post-natal period (NMC, 2019). Midwives practise autonomously, meaning that a pregnant woman may not need or see any other health professional throughout their childbirth journey. In an uncomplicated pregnancy, the midwife's clinical decision making is conducted using a partnership approach between the pregnant woman and the midwife, which ensures a highly personalised approach to care. The role and scope of the midwife is defined by Renfrew et al (2014) in the Lancet series on midwifery as:

> *Skilled, knowledgeable, and compassionate care for childbearing women, newborn infants, and families across the continuum throughout pre-pregnancy, pregnancy, birth, postpartum, and the early weeks of life. Core characteristics include optimising normal biological, psychological, social, and cultural processes of reproduction and early life; timely prevention and management of complications; consultation with and referral to other services; respect for women's individual circumstances and views; and working in partnership with women to strengthen women's own capabilities to care for themselves and their families.*
>
> (Renfrew et al, 2014, p 1130)

Understandably, not all pregnancies are uncomplicated, and midwives need to be skilled in working within and across multi-professional and multi-agency teams (NMC, 2019). For example, a woman with a long-term medical condition may be supported by a medical team with care delivered through a maternal medicine hub. Within this model however, the central point of contact remains the midwife. The model of decision making in this type of care should also reflect a partnership approach and is often described as *'woman centred'*, *'person centred'* or *'family centred'*.

Midwifery in the United Kingdom (UK) at the time of writing is undergoing a turbulent time. The *Better Births* report (NHS England, 2016) made recommendations for change to the way in which maternity care is delivered, including the allocation of funding. Subsequently, the national Maternity Transformation Programme (NHS England, 2017) which followed drew together practice partners across the NHS to implement changes for safer personalised care. Ten workstreams were launched, including a model of continuity of carer, personalised care funding which follows the woman through midwifery services, digital transformation for maternity systems and changes to the workforce skill mix. Progress on these workstreams was unfortunately interrupted by the global Covid-19 pandemic, which impacted the health service severely between 2020 and 2022. A review by Ockenden (2022) of current and historic maternity cases of stillbirth, neonatal morbidity and maternal death in one NHS Trust in England has focused government and public attention on the shortcomings of maternity care and the urgent need for this review's recommendations to be implemented across England. Essentially, Ockenden's 2022 findings demonstrated poor decisions by midwives and obstetricians within flawed systems of care; ultimately, these poor decisions had devastating consequences for families. Midwives have consequently found themselves in the middle of a critical media storm; their decision making and their approach to professional partnership working with obstetricians is under the spotlight. As a profession we are embracing the recommended changes and learning from feedback on the services we provide.

This book is an opportunity to highlight the incredible skilled decision making, complexity and range of midwifery practice in the UK today. We have included examples of typical dilemmas and decision making that midwives face on a regular basis to assist in preparing you for working with birthing women and people, families and other professionals. As you will see, midwives not only provide support and guidance but use their knowledge and networks to enable safe birthing, keeping a clear focus on the humane aspects of the experience of transitioning to parenting.

The book is divided into three parts: the first part relates to experiences and concerns for safe and effective care, the definition of which may differ depending on your point of view. Women and pregnant people may be accepting of a risk which may not be acceptable to the system in which midwives work. This is explored in the experiences of Samia, Imogen and Martha in which midwives work through the decisions in approaching birth from a different world view. The second part expresses the dilemmas midwives face in prioritising care, including the experience of supporting student midwives, examining issues of safe staffing and care delivery when difficult conversations are needed. The concluding part of the book explores the role of the midwife and the decisions they take in personalising care for a refugee and her family (Rahaf), a trans man Oli and Lucy, who gave birth during the isolating time of Covid lockdown.

How to use this book

This book can be read in several ways. For example, you can read it in the order it is written, or you can simply dip in and out of clinical scenarios that match your learning requirements at the time. Each case study starts with a fictitious clinical scenario told from the perspective of the midwife. These scenarios provide an insight into the various aspects of midwifery practice and imparts the midwife's thinking through evidence, theories, models or concepts (presented as 'shoutouts') that enable them to appraise options and make a sound clinical decision. The clinical scenarios also include the midwife's reflections either in action (while it is happening) or on action (after the event), providing further insight into how clinical decisions must evolve based on the evidence available. Subsequently, a set of reflective questions is provided to enable you as a reader to consider your own knowledge and learning. We hope that you will find the questions stimulating and that you take the opportunity to read further. In anticipation that you will want to relate your reading to your own clinical practice, we have provided some suggestions for reading and resources to help. We would encourage you to work with either a peer or clinical supervisor to ensure you expose yourself to a variety of differing perspectives and analyse what you may or may not have done differently. By scrutinising and reflecting on day-to-day practice, you will understand the importance of being able to justify to multiple audiences exactly why you made the specific decisions you did.

References

NHS England (2016) *National Maternity Review. Better Births: Improving Outcomes of Maternity Services in England – A Five Year Forward View for Maternity Care*. [online] Available at: www.england.nhs.uk/wp-content/uploads/2016/02/national-maternity-review-report.pdf (accessed 19 December 2022).

NHS England (2017) Maternity Transformation Programme. [online] Available at: www.england.nhs.uk/mat-transformation (accessed 9 March 2023).

Nursing & Midwifery Council (NMC) (2019) *Standards of Proficiency for Midwives*. [online] Available at: www.nmc.org.uk/globalassets/sitedocuments/standards/standards-of-proficiency-for-midwives.pdf (accessed 23 January 2023).

Ockenden, D (2022) *Findings, Conclusions and Essential Actions from the Independent Review of Maternity Services at The Shrewsbury and Telford Hospital NHS Trust*. London: HMSO.

Renfrew, M, McFadden A, Bastos, M H and Campbell J et al (2014) Midwifery and Quality Care: Findings from a New Evidence Informed Framework for Maternal and Newborn Care. *The Lancet*, 384: 1129– 45.

Part 1

Universal and additional care: risk and safety

Case study 1
Samia: my world view is not the same as yours

Ella Caine and Kenda Crozier

Introduction

This case study explores the dilemmas encountered when standardised maternity service practices are at odds with the personal preferences of individual users of the service, particularly in cases where individuals are from minoritised racial or ethnic groups. It touches upon current problems of inequality of service provision and outcome, which have been the focus of several contemporary reviews and reports, most notably *The Black Maternity Experiences Survey* report (2022), Birthrights UK's *Systemic Racism, Not Broken Bodies* (2022), and the report on *Maternity Experiences of Muslim Women from Racialised Minority Communities* (2022). With these reports in mind, this case study explores the challenges that may arise when world views between midwives and families differ. The need to acknowledge and respect spiritual and cultural beliefs in the context of pregnancy is examined through the example of a woman whose own belief system resists the recommendation of additional treatment options.

Samia's story

Samia is a 25 year-old woman and pregnant for the first time. She is a British Muslim of Dominican heritage. She and her husband, Adam, are excited about the pregnancy but also apprehensive about negotiating a health system with which they have had little previous contact. Samia works as a broker for a large insurance company and has a degree in accountancy. Adam works in a different department at the same company as a computer analyst. They have been married for four years. Her pregnancy has been straightforward and she has attended all antenatal appointments but has developed high blood pressure in

MODEL: Birmingham Symptom Specific Obstetric Triage System (BSOTS) (Kenyon et al, 2017) has been adopted by the Trust. In this system, midwives carry out a standardised assessment of each woman attending triage within 15 minutes of arrival. Women are then categorised according to one of four levels of urgency; this guides timing of subsequent standardised immediate care for the eight most common reasons for attendance

the third trimester and her community midwife has referred her to the local maternity assessment unit (MAU) where she can be triaged. She feels nervous about going alone and calls Adam at work, asking him to go with her for moral support. They get to the MAU 50 minutes after the arrangement was made. They are welcomed by the ward clerk, who takes Samia's handheld summary notes from her and they are then shown to a waiting room. A sign on the wall says that the average initial waiting time that day is 15 minutes. Though the waiting room is full of other people, it is silent. Samia hopes they won't have to be too long so that Adam can get back to work but is glad she is not alone. Within minutes she is called into another area, a compact single room full of medical equipment. A midwife, Leonie, and a maternity support worker (MSW), Serena, are present. They are both white. In fact, since Samia arrived she has seen no one else who looks like her. They introduce themselves. Leonie asks Samia what has brought her to the unit and asks whether Serena can check her 'obs'. Samia does not know what 'obs' means but quickly learns that her blood pressure and other vital signs are to be assessed. Samia is also asked to provide a clean urine sample. Leonie enquires about her baby's movements, which Samia tells her have been the same as normal. Leonie listens to the fetal heart with a handheld Doppler and comments that the baseline is within a normal range, and that there are accelerations: healthy signs. However, Samia's blood pressure is still high. Leonie explains that she wants to do some other checks. Samia agrees to these tests, although reluctantly. Even though the midwife is kind and explains things to her in a way she can understand, Samia feels she has become engulfed in a system which is moving too fast for her. She wonders whether her blood pressure is affected by the discomfort she feels about being in an unfamiliar environment. She asks if she can go home and return tomorrow. Adam also feels out of his depth but is worried something may be wrong. Leonie is puzzled about Samia's concerns and asks her to walk her through her thinking, which reveals a world about which the local maternity service has little knowledge.

VALUES: informed choice, communication, locus of control, social model of childbirth

Samia's medical condition is recognised: the midwife's story

I was the midwife looking after Samia in the MAU of a large teaching hospital. It was a busy shift, but Samia was seen for an initial assessment within the standard 15 minutes. She came with her husband, Adam, having been referred by her community midwife for high blood pressure at her routine appointment. Samia was 32 weeks (about seven and a half months) pregnant, feeling well with no symptoms of raised blood pressure. She is Black British, as is Adam. The MSW has assessed her vital signs. Samia's temperature was 36.8°C. She had a pulse of 80 bpm, a respiratory rate of 14 pm, and blood pressure of 152/100 mmHg. Oxygen saturation via pulse oximetry was 99 per cent in air. This gave her a modified early warning score (MEWS) of 4, prompting the need for an obstetric review within 30 minutes, and continuous electronic fetal monitoring (CEFM). As part of this assessment, Samia had been asked to provide a clean urine sample which, when tested, contained 1 + protein. I knew that the raised blood pressure and proteinuria were signs of pre-eclampsia and that we would need more evidence from blood tests.

Samia has not had much, if any, experience of 'traditional' healthcare as throughout her life she and her family have often relied on complementary therapies and diet to control ailments and illnesses. I explain to Samia and Adam that the signs of high blood pressure and protein in her urine sample were pointing to either gestational hypertension or a condition called pre-eclampsia, but more tests would be needed to confirm this. Samia has heard of pre-eclampsia through her reading but did not think it would apply to someone as healthy as she is.

Pre-eclampsia is complicated. There is always a dilemma between giving information that could scare women, such as the risk of seizures or a stroke, and giving proper unbiased information to help women decide what they want to do. In the workplace we are constantly reminded of the 'Montgomery Ruling', and how we must give women

EVIDENCE: the National Institute for Health and Care Excellence (NICE, 2019) guidelines on hypertension in pregnancy define pre-eclampsia as new onset of hypertension (over 140 mmHg systolic or over 90 mmHg diastolic) after 20 weeks of pregnancy and the coexistence of one or more of the following new-onset conditions: proteinuria or other maternal organ dysfunction

EVIDENCE: early warning scoring systems are a tool to detect decline in condition of a patient before it becomes so serious that it is irreversible. The parameters for detection are altered in pregnancy, hence the need for a specialist scoring tool

MODEL: locus of control

VALUE: complementary alternative therapies

THEORY: Montgomery
Judgement (Montgomery v
Lanarkshire Health Board, 2015)

EVIDENCE: Liu et al (2022)
presented contrasting theory
about a cardiac cause

EVIDENCE: BSOTS (Kenyon
et al, 2017)

information that is important to them rather than what we feel they should know.

I explain how pre-eclampsia is usually linked to a problem with placental function, although the cause is not fully understood. Because it can affect vital organs, I want to take blood samples, test how well her liver and kidneys are working, and check the protein level in a urine sample. I also want to check on her baby using electronic fetal monitoring. When the results of the tests become available, I plan to discuss them with the obstetrician, who will decide with Samia what to do next. These actions are based on following treatment algorithms developed specifically for maternity triage services. In my experience, it may also include Samia being recommended medication to reduce her blood pressure. Samia appears confused about why these actions are indicated. She does not feel sick and is not concerned about her baby, whose movements are as frequent and regular as they normally are. She accepts the moderate risk factor of this being her first pregnancy, but the picture I am painting does not fit what she feels about herself.

I ask her if there are any reasons that she does not want me to investigate her blood pressure any further; I really want to understand her point of view and offer any information I can do to help her make sense of her situation. Samia hesitantly shares with me that she has limited faith in the healthcare system and has a somewhat negative view of hospital care; her cousin had recently died due to sepsis, which had not been recognised in its initial stages leading to a delay in effecting a response. Samia feels that the care her cousin received had somehow contributed to their death. She tells me that although other people in her community may react differently, her own Muslim belief means that she looks beyond worldly dimensions for answers to life problems, believing that things will work out in the way that they are supposed to for her and her family. She finds it hard to relate to the idea that she is ill and may deteriorate, but after our discussion agrees to these investigations, albeit without any eagerness. Because of the MEWS score she has an initial assessment with an obstetrician, and further tests are done

EVIDENCE: placental growth factor-based testing (PLGF), a blood test (NICE, 2022)

I appreciate that others may have different views from my own. I have previously ensured I take the time to look into what others' beliefs and rituals may be around their choices in pregnancy and for birth. However, I feel a little out of my depth in this context because in my experience women do not often question care when it is related to the safety of themselves or their unborn baby. It makes me nervous that Samia would consider declining treatment for something medically recognised as so serious.

I tell Samia and Adam that they will have more information from the tests soon, and that I must go and attend to other families until then. I reassure them that I will be back once she has had a review. I show them back into the waiting room and share my findings with the lead midwife who will organise the obstetric review. Upon my return, Samia's investigation results have been seen by the obstetric registrar and a diagnosis is made of pre-eclampsia from the abnormal results of her liver and kidney function, and urine tests. Her PLGF test result is also abnormal, suggesting placental dysfunction but that Samia is not at an increased risk of pre-term birth (PLGF between 12pg/ml and 99 pg/ml).

MODEL: obstetric-led care

EVIDENCE: PLGF-based testing to help diagnose suspected pre-eclampsia (NICE, 2022)

Samia has been advised to remain in the hospital as an inpatient for observation, and so that treatment for pre-eclampsia can be started. Although it would have been possible for her to be discharged home, the registrar has recommended she stays for observation. I transfer her to the antenatal ward. Adam leaves to return to work; Samia and I have a little time to talk while we are walking over together, and she vocalises her concerns. '*Surely it is up to me; it should be my decision whether I take the medication or not? I am not ill, or at least I do not feel as though I am. I am a professional woman; that must mean they know I am a sensible person and would not risk something so precious as my own baby!*'

EVIDENCE: Liu et al (2022) found that by altering the standard screening process in pregnancy to a new tool and providing targeted intervention, the risks of perinatal deaths in black and minority ethnic women could be reduced from more than three times greater to equivalence with white women

Samia tells me that the obstetrician did not spend very much time explaining why everyone was so worried. I try to explain to her that because we know the risk of poor outcomes in pregnancy are higher for black and minority ethnic women, the health service is now trying to ensure we make active treatment decisions and intervene earlier when we see there is a risk.

It is busy today and I give a brief handover to one of the antenatal ward midwives, stating the plan is to commence anti-hypertensive treatment as soon as possible. As I settle Samia in her allocated bed space, she says she would like to speak to her family before she starts the medication.

As a midwife, I cannot understand why she came to the hospital if she is not prepared to accept advice and recommendations, or even a diagnosis. I feel confused about why Samia wants to delay starting treatment for her condition. However, I suppose it is reasonable that she wants to ask her family, who are part of her support network, and I leave her to have the conversations she wants to. I feel the need to discuss this with the registrar and take some advice about what I should do. I feel concerned but need to get back to MAU. The senior midwife at the desk, who is of white British origin, has overheard the conversation between Samia and me. As I leave the ward having settled Samia, she says: *'Why are these people always so difficult? Can't she see that she is endangering the baby; what a silly woman. Don't they know? No wonder that they are more likely to have bad outcomes in pregnancy.'* What I don't do is respond immediately by countering the senior midwife's comments, although they disturb me. I was not sure whether they were racist comments, but I knew they amounted to stereotyping people based on their race or ethnicity. I thought about how those opinions could affect the way midwives care for women and families. I wondered whether some of the lack of trust which Samia had discussed with me was influenced by experiencing discriminatory care or hearing about it from others. I had also heard similar comments from other midwives and did not think anything I did would make a difference.

EVIDENCE: Birthrights summarise different ways racism is manifested (eg systemic, institutional, interpersonal) in their report Systemic Racism, Not Broken Bodies (2022)

EVIDENCE: The Care Quality Commission (2021) identified from hospital episode statistics that there was a disparity in pregnancy outcomes between white women and black and minority ethnic women

I return to the antenatal ward soon after to transfer another woman from MAU. Samia is not in her bed space when I go to see her, and one of the other ward midwives points to the day room. I go to the day room. Samia is there with her bag. She tells me she will go home and has decided not to take the medication now. She has some other options she wants to look into first, including complementary therapies. She also wants to discuss this with Adam and other family members. I feel dismayed and I wonder whether I am to blame for not being firmer in advising Samia to have the medication. I need to ask the obstetric registrar to discuss this with her before she goes. Luckily for me, she agrees to wait for this. I arrange for this conversation and nervously inform the senior midwife.

> *MODEL: MDT (multi-disciplinary team) working, informed consent, protective steering*

Reflections

I have taken an interest in health inequalities in general, and maternal inequalities in particular, because I honestly believe that how we treat the least advantaged tells us more about our performance and values than how the most advantaged experience care. There is a plethora of evidence and literature about health inequalities now, but the catalyst for my interest was learning about health outcomes for black and Asian people from the NHS Race and Health Observatory report (2022). The findings of this report were difficult to read. I have not been aware of situations where women have been discriminated against because of their race or ethnicity in the service. However, it occurs to me that not having personal knowledge does not mean that there is no problem, and women may not always be comfortable making complaints about such issues.

Actions

I am going to make a point of doing more to increase my understanding of maternal health inequalities. Having read *The Black Maternity Experiences Survey* report published on the FIVEXMORE website, I am aware that there is a lack of sensitivity in the way some health professionals address women and there is also a lack of knowledge about anatomy and physiology, with many misconceptions about minority ethnic bodies. Reading the stories of women's experience of healthcare in *The Black Maternity Experiences Survey* report is a starting point for me. The survey provides some action points, which I am determined to champion in my organisation. There seems to be a general awareness of risks but the communication with women and communities is still not as good as it could be. I am committed to being a safe practitioner, where my actions contribute to greater equity and do not cause harm. Having come across the concept of cultural safety, adopted in countries such as New Zealand, where it is the indigenous people who are more at risk of poor outcomes, I would like to explore it as a tool to improve my local service. I will also try to engage with the Trust's Maternity Voices Partnership to see what commitments there are to working with all local populations.

EVIDENCE: the concept of cultural safety has been contrasted with cultural competence (Curtis et al, 2019)

Questions for reflection and discussion

1. There is no simple solution to the dilemma of a woman whose world view is different from the medical view of a maternal condition. What steps would you take in this situation? Is there guidance you would use to help with your practice?

2. Read and reflect on the report from Birthrights in the helpful resources section of this case study – are there any changes you might make to your own practice and how might you go about making them?

3. What actions would you take if you witness or are informed about racist or discriminatory comments or practices from health professionals? What systems are in place in your organisation that could advise you?

4. What are the possible outcomes of the case discussed above?

5. Consider how you seek the views of women when you offer options for care – are there any changes you can make to ensure that their views are effectively heard?

6. How can maternity care organisations work more closely with minoritised/marginalised communities to ensure safe care for all women?

Helpful resources

Birthrights report (2022) *Systemic Racism, Not Broken Bodies* – www.birthrights.org.uk/wp-content/uploads/2022/05/Birthrights-inquiry-systemic-racism_exec-summary_May-22-web.pdf

Muslim Woman's Network UK: *INVISIBLE Maternity Experiences of Muslim Women from Racialised Minority Communities* – www.mwnuk.co.uk/go_files/resources/maternity_report_120722.pdf

Royal College of Midwives: *Informed Decision Making* –www.rcm.org.uk/media/6007/informed-decision-making_0604.pdf

The Black Maternity Experiences Survey report – www.fivexmore.com

Professor Thilaganthan describes placental dysfunction. TED talk – http://bit.ly/2i1SqDk

References

Care Quality Commission (2021) Safety, Equity and Engagement in Maternity Services. [online] Available at: www.cqc.org.uk/publications/themes-care/safety-equity-engagement-maternity-services#intro (accessed 19 December 2022).

Curtis, E, Jones, R, Tipene- Leach, D, Walker, C, Loring, B, Paine, S J and Reid P (2019) Why Cultural Safety Rather Than Cultural Competency Is Required to Achieve Health Equity: A Literature Review and Recommended Definition. [online] Available at: https://equity healthj.biomedcentral.com/articles/10.1186/s12939-019-1082-3 (accessed 19 December 2022).

Kenyon, S, Hewison, A, Dann, S-A, Easterbrook, J, Hamilton-Giachritsis, C, Beckmann, A and Johns, N (2017) The Design and Implementation of an Obstetric Triage System for Unscheduled Pregnancy Related Attendances: A Mixed Methods Evaluation. *BMC Pregnancy and Childbirth*, 17: 309.

Liu, B, Nadeem, U, Frick, A, Morakinyo, A, Bhida, A and Thilaganathan, B (2022) Reducing Health Inequality in Black, Asian and Other Minority Ethnic Pregnant Women: Impact of First Trimester Combined Screening for Placental Dysfunction on Perinatal Mortality. *BJOG*, 129: 1750–6.

Montgomery v Lanarkshire Health Board (2015) Judgment given on 11 March 205. Supreme Court. [online] Available at: www.supremecourt.uk/cases/docs/uksc-2013-0136-judgment.pdf (accessed 7 April 2023).

National Institute for Health and Care Excellence (NICE) (2019) Hypertension in Pregnancy: Diagnosis and Management. [online] Available at: www.nice.org.uk/guidance/ng133/resources/hypertension-in-pregnancy-diagnosis-and-management-pdf-66141717671365 (accessed 1 December 2022).

National Institute for Health and Care Excellence (NICE) (2022) PLGF-based Testing to Help Diagnose Suspected Preterm Pre-eclampsia. Diagnostic Guidance 49. [online] Available at: www.nice.org.uk/guidance/dg49/resources/plgfbased-testing-to-help-diagnose-suspected-preterm-preeclampsia-pdf (accessed 11 January 2023).

NHS Race and Health Observatory (2022) *Mapping Existing Policy Interventions to Tackle Ethnic Health Inequalities in Maternal and Neonatal Health in England: A Systematic Scoping Review with Stakeholder Engagement.* [online] Available at: www.nhsrho.org/wp-content/uploads/2022/12/RHO-Mapping-existing-policy-interventions_December-2022.pdf (accessed 18 December 2022).

Case study 2
Imogen: swimming against the tide

Jemma Thorne and Ruth Sanders

Introduction

This case study explores the challenges midwives may face when managing situations which they have only previously encountered during simulated scenarios. By focusing on the support midwives provide when facilitating a vaginal breech birth, aspects of more unusual care are examined, including the challenges this can provoke in the wider multi-disciplinary team alongside the midwife's role as advocate. Inherent caring bias is considered throughout this case study and self-reflection surrounding fully informed consent is examined. The case study closes with ideas for further actions to develop reflective skills, together with suggestions for evidence-based enquiry and supportive exploration with colleagues.

EVIDENCE: Royal College of Obstetricians and Gynaecologist guidance states that 'The presence of a skilled birth attendant is essential for a safe vaginal breech birth' (Impey et al, 2017b). Because only 3–4 per cent of pregnancies have breech-presenting fetuses at term, there is little exposure for professionals to experience facilitating vaginal breech birth outside training situations (Shuttler, 2018)

Night shift on the delivery suite

It is 03:08 on the night shift and I see the delivery suite co-ordinator approach as I am finishing writing my notes. She tells me that Imogen, a 28 year-old primigravida, carrying a confirmed breech baby, wants a vaginal birth and is on her way into the unit. As an experienced band 6 midwife, within the skill mix tonight I am the most appropriate midwife to be allocated for this individual. As I wait for Imogen to arrive, I mentally prepare for what is to come next. I have witnessed vaginal breech births with positive outcomes but have not been the responsible midwife in charge of the care. I feel the familiar pang of anxiety in my stomach, adrenaline kicking in. There is a senior specialist registrar on duty at the desk and she looks up as I walk pass, smiles and says she sees that a woman is on her way into the unit with a breech-presenting baby; I smile back and tell her I will let her know when I have assessed her.

THEORY: professional competence

THEORY: autonomous practice, professional scope

MODEL: additional care needs in labour, role of the midwife

THEORY: psychological safety. Midwifery work is often perceived externally as a joyful vocation, but there is a growing body of work which acknowledges the psychological impact of caring for individuals in complex caring situations, experiencing pain, anxiety and stress (Pezaro et al, 2016)

MODEL: multi-disciplinary working for additional care needs in labour

I prepare the room and the equipment I know I will need. The delivery trolley in the corner of the room is ready and as I check the resuscitaire, I think back to the shocked faces of the vaginal breech babies I have witnessed.

At 03:44 Imogen arrives at the delivery suite with her partner, Peter. I meet them at the door and introduce myself. Imogen looks up at me but soon leans on Peter when a contraction arrives. She sways her hips and breathes steadily. At first glance, she appears in advanced labour. As the contraction ends and her senses awaken to her surroundings, we start to walk down the corridor to her room. I nod silently at the co-ordinator as we walk past as a non-verbal acknowledgement of Imogen's arrival.

The big delivery room is clinical, a delivery bed in the middle of the room with a resuscitaire in the corner. I have kept the lights low with the bedside lamp and resuscitaire emitting their glow to create a calm environment encouraging release of oxytocin. In between contractions, I explain to Imogen and Peter that there is a bedpan in the toilet and ask if Imogen can provide a urine sample for me. I hold the bedside buzzer up to them both and show them how to use it if I am outside the room. I leave them for a few moments to adapt to their unfamiliar environment, to provide a urine sample and to allow me time to read Imogen's maternity notes.

Outside the room I read the handheld notes. Imogen is a primigravida, 41 weeks, blood group is rhesus positive, haemoglobin is in normal range, ultrasound scans and growth chart as expected. Imogen would be described as having universal care in her pregnancy until her breech presentation was confirmed at 36 weeks. There is documentation of a discussion between the obstetrician and Imogen regarding external cephalic version, the risks and statistics of proceeding with a vaginal breech along with the option of an elective caesarean section. Imogen declined both the external cephalic version and the elective caesarean section. Further documentation at both 38 weeks and 40 weeks reiterates the risk factors of vaginal breech. I read Imogen and Peter's birth preferences and

---

VALUE: interprofessional communication. The delivery suite co-ordinator role is vital in creating a safe environment, providing oversight of midwifery working practices and liaising with obstetric staff (Bunford and Hamilton, 2019). Evidence suggests that communication with the co-ordinator is a crucial aspect of situational awareness, and this can be expressed in different forms such as non-verbal communication

THEORY: birth environment. Oxytocin is a neuropeptide which has significant impact on social interaction (Hammond et al, 2013). The production and release of oxytocin can be initiated by the experiences and perception of environmental factors, making the birth space a highly sensitive environment (Goldkuhl et al, 2022). Individuals need to feel safe for spontaneous labour to progress, and oxytocin assists this process by reducing stress, increasing calm and promoting positive interpersonal relationships (Hammond et al, 2013)

VALUES: respect, confidentiality

EVIDENCE: Many women report that discussions about birth options for breech are primarily between women and obstetricians, with the midwifery voice less apparent (Sierra, 2021)

EVIDENCE: Impey et al (2017a, 2017b)

VALUE: informed choice. The Code (NMC, 2018) states that in order to 'act in the best interests of people at all times', it is important for midwives to obtain 'properly informed consent' and to have documented this prior to any action being carried out in the course of providing care

recognise familiar requests such as preferring Entonox if needed and to avoid an epidural. There is no mention of the baby being breech in this section of the notes.

Entering Imogen's room, I note the bathroom door is wide open and Imogen has changed into a nightdress. Peter looks anxious. Imogen's demeanour is strong and confident, and I can see she is trusting and listening to her body. I ask if I can perform her observations and follow her around the room to take her blood pressure, pulse, temperature and respiratory rate.

To perform an abdominal palpation, I ask Imogen to lie on the bed; she is happy to do so, reporting that fetal movements have been normal today and that she last felt the baby move when driving into the hospital. Her membranes ruptured at 02:30, pink in colour and continuing to drain; her contractions have been every two to three minutes for the last hour. As I palpate her abdomen, I recognise the hard presenting part near her fundus, confirming with the handheld scanner that the baby remains breech. This is the first time we discuss presentation; her eyes tell me this is not a discussion she wants to have again. I explain the recommendation for continuous electronic fetal monitoring, and she consents. Imogen is keen to know her progress; all non-verbal signals tell me her labour is reaching the last stage. I offer a vaginal examination, which she accepts. On examination I feel a frank breech and a thin anterior lip of cervix; I explain my findings. After explaining my findings, Imogen and Peter are clearly delighted that the labour is advancing so well and that they were able to stay at home in their own environment for most of it. The cardiotocograph (CTG) continues and has been on for around ten minutes; it is reassuring: baseline is 150 bpm, with a single acceleration noted, no decelerations and good variability. I document my notes thus far in the corner of the room, knowing that the birth will not be long.

EVIDENCE: the Code (NMC, 2018) states that midwives should 'avoid making assumptions and recognise diversity and individual choice' (prioritise people 1.3)

EVIDENCE: RCOG suggests that while evidence is lacking in this area, 'continuous fetal monitoring may lead to improved neonatal outcomes' (NICE, 2017)

THEORY: informed consent

VALUES: compassion, women-centred care

MODEL: emotional support from labour companion (WHO, 2018)

After the vaginal examination I encourage Imogen to listen to her body; she steps off the bed and sways her hips. I explain that if Imogen wants any analgesia, she should let me know and I can arrange this for her. She nods in recognition of my words, signalling to me she is okay. I explain to them both my need to leave the room to update the team on her progress. I will be out for a brief time, but if needed they must press the call bell. Peter nods and smiles at me. I explain to the co-ordinator that Imogen has an anterior rim of cervix left and I need to get back to the room urgently. She tells me she will update the registrar and let the neonatal team know and that I should buzz if I need anything.

EVIDENCE: multi-disciplinary communication

When I walk back into the room, Imogen is more vocal than when I left. As her next contraction arrives, I recognise the sound of an early deceleration indicated by a drop in the baseline of over 15 bpm for more than 15 seconds on the CTG. She is pleased I have returned and climbs onto the bed, adopting a position she wants to be in. I explain I have updated the midwifery co-ordinator and she will let the rest of the team know, and they will introduce themselves to her shortly. Her eyes fill with trepidation, and I offer reassurance that she is doing well and to continue listening to her body. As per Trust guidelines, I offer an antacid and cannula, explaining the risk of aspiration if she has to be taken to theatre and the need to obtain venous access for blood tests and to give Imogen intravenous drugs in an emergency. Imogen declines the antacid but accepts the cannula. I cannulate, take bloods, flushing the cannula, and apply a dressing between contractions.

VALUE: dignity

THEORY: informed consent

With the next contraction Imogen involuntarily pushes, her body working for itself and taking the lead. I check under the sheet and recognise physiological clues of the second stage approaching: anal dilation, vulval gaping and a stretch on the perineum. I explain to Imogen and Peter that I will be buzzing to request assistance as I press the call bell.

MODEL: midwifery-led care

The midwifery co-ordinator and obstetric registrars walk in and introduce themselves. Imogen has another contraction and bears down, vulval gaping widening with a glimpse of the presenting part and some fresh meconium. So far, the CTG continues with no concerns. At this point the

Dilemmas and Decision Making in Midwifery

senior and junior registrar reach Imogen's bedside and look her directly in the eyes. They tell Imogen she is doing well and ask if she has considered a caesarean section. Imogen's eyes dart across to me; I do not feel the need to say anything as Imogen is strong enough to verbalise her needs, but I know from her eye contact that she wants me on side. Another contraction takes over her body before she gets the chance to answer and she bears down; I encourage her to listen to her body and to go with it. The senior registrar looks across at me, while I continue to look directly at Imogen. Once the contraction has passed, the registrar says to continue towards a vaginal birth because Imogen's labour is now too advanced for a caesarean.

At this point, as much as I want to advocate for Imogen, I feel my own fight or flight response activate and note my high heart rate, dry mouth, clammy hands and need to step from one foot to the other continuously. I hope nobody in the room has noticed, and I portray a sense of calm. I am aware the next stages of the birth are time critical and do not want the baby to be deprived of oxygen or stimulate the cord in any way.

The registrar asks me to take off the end of the delivery bed and put Imogen's legs into lithotomy, which is what I have practised in the emergency training for breech birth. Imogen is happy with this position and continues to bear down with the next contraction. The senior registrar stands next to me at the bottom of the bed, with her junior behind her. I make my body as wide as possible, adopting a super-hero pose, making it clear I will be responsible for the birth, advocating for Imogen. Both registrars respectfully keep their distance.

Imogen listens to her body's urges and the presenting part advances, both buttocks advance, quickly followed by the back. I hear the junior registrar whisper to the senior registrar, asking her if I should be doing more. The senior registrar tells her I am doing exactly what I should be. At this stage, the CTG becomes irrelevant, and the delivery suite co-ordinator subtly removes the transducers from

EVIDENCE: evidence focused on individual experience suggests that there can be a bias around institutional or practitioner preferences regarding the management of breech presentation conversations (Morris et al, 2022). Trust guidelines should enable a collaborative discussion promoting informed consent through utilising evidence-based best practice approaches that avoid coercive or pressurised language, instead offering a full range of choice (Impey et al, 2017b)

THEORY: territorial behaviour. There is evidence suggesting that when a midwife is providing one-to-one care and the birth environment changes from midwife-led to the labour ward, territorial behaviours can manifest in 'us versus them' behaviour (Sosa, 2018)

MODEL: collaborative working, simulation training. It is acknowledged that there may be different practitioner preferences to facilitating vaginal breech birth and that to develop expertise it is important to work in 'breech teams' to ensure that choice is truly offered (Spillane, 2020)

EVIDENCE: hormonal response. Carney et al's study (2010, p 1364) demonstrated that there were 'increased levels of testosterone, decreases in cortisol and increased feelings of power and tolerance for risk' in those individuals who assumed an open high-power non-verbal pose

Imogen's abdomen. The room is filled with silence briefly before the next contraction arrives.

I continue to encourage Imogen to listen to her body and feel encouraged by the reassurance of the senior doctor in the room. With the next contraction the right leg delivers, followed shortly by the left leg. Imogen continues to push, and the right shoulder and arm deliver followed by the left shoulder and arm. So far, I have not needed to touch the baby. Throughout this stage of labour, I continue to encourage Imogen to listen to her body and keep the room calm. Sensing my need for instruction, the senior registrar advises me how to hold the baby to help deliver the baby's head. I follow her instructions implicitly and with the next contraction the baby arrives.

The baby is pale, eyes wide open and not breathing. I stimulate the baby by rubbing her back; her eyes are wide and blinking, shocked by her arrival in the world. I was extra diligent when checking the resuscitaire, knowing that Imogen's baby, because of its presentation, may be more likely to need resuscitation. Counselling about birth mode should include reference to the fact that planned vaginal breech increases the chances of lower Apgar scores as well as short-term complications. However, evidence does not suggest any longer-term morbidities (RCOG, 2017). As I hand the baby to the paediatrician she cries for the first time, a sound the room is pleased to hear. Following a brief examination on the rescusitaire, the baby is brought to Imogen for skin to skin. Imogen and Peter are lost in oxytocin.

Reflections

Before Imogen arrived, I was hopeful the baby had turned into the cephalic presentation since the last assessment. Breech presentation occurs in 3–4 per cent of all term neonates and a larger proportion of pre-term neonates. The current evidence suggests that there is a 50 per cent chance of an external cephalic version (ECV) being successful and the RCOG recommend that women be informed that ECV can reduce their chances of having a

> **THEORY: psychological safety.** Psychological safety is present when colleagues trust and respect each other and feel able – even obligated – to be candid (Edmondson, 2019)

caesarean section (Impey et al, 2017a). When I confirmed that Imogen's baby was still breech, I realised that although I felt anxious about the prospect of caring for a woman with a breech presentation, I felt privileged to be able to apply my training to practice, ensuring that Imogen had midwifery-led care.

VALUES: continued professional development, competent practice

Would I pursue a vaginal birth if my own baby were in the breech presentation? I questioned whether Imogen would change her mind and request a caesarean section. Having witnessed obstetric discussion previously, I understand the risks of vaginal breech need to be discussed but feel saddened by the communication around statistics and can imagine the fear factor Imogen would have felt in these discussions. I wonder what Imogen's reasons were for feeling so strongly about declining both ECV and an elective caesarean section. I should have tried to converse further with her about her choices when she arrived. I wonder if I could have approached this in more detail; was I protecting Imogen rather than actively involving her in her decision? I feel frustrated that caesarean was mentioned casually at a time when a decision had already been made.

THEORY: maternal choice and decision making

MODEL: cross disciplinary working, midwifery scope of practice

VALUE: midwifery guardianship

In retrospect, I see the reason I chose not to make explicit my level of experience was because I wanted to convey confidence to Imogen, the obstetric team but also in myself and my practice. I trained for this situation and have the skills to lead her care and worried that if I divulged my insecurity then I might have experienced a loss of faith in my own ability and conveyed this to Imogen and my colleagues.

THEORY: territorial behaviour

MODEL: midwifery leadership

VALUE: professional communication

Actions

I feel empowered to lead and want to consolidate this and in time support others with their confidence in this skill. I acknowledge that this was a learning opportunity for the multi-professional team, as incidence of breech is low, and afterwards I chose to share my experience with other midwives to encourage them to explore the evidence beyond Trust guidelines to support physiological breech birth. I will seek out further debriefing with the obstetric team to discuss my management and explore other opportunities where I can take the lead in situations in which I am less familiar with the guidance and support.

I have realised that there were several aspects to my care for Imogen that, as a midwife, I intuitively assumed. I advocated for Imogen, reading non-verbal cues regarding her wishes, and adopted a protective position when facilitating her birth. Communication entailed reading verbal and non-verbal cues, but in future I want to explore a more direct discussion about breech presentation without making assumptions from the cues and my intuition.

MODEL: Schwartz rounds provide an opportunity for staff to revisit their values, enhance peer support and promote compassionate caring practice with group reflective discussions on challenging experiences. Maben et al (2021) demonstrated positive improvements in organisational change and an improvement in teamwork from this practice

I did not say anything to the registrar at the time about her questioning Imogen on her choice of delivery. Although I felt supported to take the lead in the situation, by introducing the idea of a caesarean to Imogen, it seemed that her choice to have a vaginal breech birth could have been undermined and she would lose her confidence in our ability to facilitate her choices as a wider team. I would like to revisit this conversation and consider how our communication could be improved in future instances by the use of a Schwartz round.

Questions for reflection and discussion

1. How would you feel about caring for a woman in a situation you have never experienced before, although you may have experienced this in a simulation?

2. Are you up to date with the most recent evidence for vaginal breech and your local Trust guidelines on how to manage vaginal breech birth? Make a list of key points for yourself.

3. How would you manage your own emotions in this clinical situation?

4. Would you prepare the birthing environment any differently when caring for a woman with additional care needs?

5. As the midwife, how might you have undertaken a further discussion about the breech presentation?

6. How would you make unbiased decisions when there are conflicting/alternate recommendations from the midwifery and obstetric team members if a physiological birth was the woman's preference?

Helpful resources

Breech Birth Network: a community interest company dedicated to increasing skills and knowledge about vaginal breech birth – https://breechbirth.org.uk

Ongoing breech research: the OptiBreech Project – https://optibreech.uk

References

Bunford, D and Hamilton, S (2019) How Delivery Suite Co-ordinators Create Situational Awareness in the Multidisciplinary Team. *British Journal of Midwifery*, 27(8): 497–505.

Carney, D R, Cuddy, A J and Yap, A J (2010) Power Posing: Brief Nonverbal Displays Affect Neuroendocrine Levels and Risk Tolerance. *Association for Psychological Science*, 21(10): 1363–8.

Edmondson, A (2019) *The Fearless Organization: Creating Psychological Safety in the Workplace for Learning, Innovation and Growth*. Hoboken, NJ: John Wiley & Sons.

Goldkuhl, L, Dellenborg, L, Berg, M, Wijk, H and Nilsson, C (2022) The Influence and Meaning of the Birth Environment for Nulliparous Women at a Hospital-based Labour Ward in Sweden: An Ethnographic Study. *Women and Birth*, 35(4): 337–47.

Hammond, A, Foreur, M, Homer, C and Davies, D (2013) Space, Place and the Midwife: Exploring the Relationship between the Birth Environment, Neurobiology and Midwifery Practice. *Women and Birth*, 26(4): 277–81.

Impey, L W M, Murphy, D J, Griffiths, M and Penna, L K on behalf of the Royal College of Obstetricians and Gynaecologists (RCOG) (2017a) External Cephalic Version and Reducing the Incidence of Term Breech Presentation. *BJOG*, 124: e178–92.

Impey, L, Murphy, D, Griffiths, M and Penna, L on behalf of the Royal College of Obstetricians and Gynaecologists (RCOG) (2017b) Management of Breech Presentation. *BJOG*, 124: e151–77.

Maben, J, Taylor, C, Reynolds, E, McCarthy, I and Leamy, M (2021) Realist Evaluation of Schwartz rounds® for Enhancing the Delivery of Compassionate Healthcare: Understanding How They Work, for Whom, and in What Contexts. *BMC Health Services Research*, 21: 709.

Morris, S, Geraghty, S and Sundin, D (2022) Breech Presentation Management: A Critical Review of Leading Clinical Practice Guidelines. *Women & Birth*, 35: e233–42.

National Institute for Health and Care Excellence (NICE) (2017) *Intrapartum Care for Healthy Women and Babies*. CG 190. London. NICE.

Nursing & Midwifery Council (NMC) (2018) *The Code: Professional Standards of Practice and Behaviour for Nurses, Midwives and Nursing Associates*. London: Nursing & Midwifery Council.

Pezaro, S, Clyne, W, Turner, A, Fulton, E and Gerada, C (2016) Midwives Overboard! Inside Their Hearts Are Breaking, Their Make-up May Be Flaking but Their Smile Still Stays On. *Women and Birth*, 29: 59–66.

Sierra, A (2021) Women's Perception of Choice and Support in Making Decisions Regarding Management of Breech Presentation. *British Journal of Midwifery*, 29(7): 392–400.

Shuttler, L (2018) Breech Birth. In Chapman, V and Charles, C (eds) *The Midwife's Labour and Birth Handbook* (pp 257–84). Hoboken, NJ: Wiley Blackwell.

Sosa, G, Crozier, K and Stockl, A (2018) The Experiences of Midwives and Women during Intrapartum Transfer from One-to-One Midwife-led Birthing Environments to Obstetric-led Units. *Midwifery*, 65: 43–50.

Spillane, E (2020) Why Breech Birth Matters. *British Journal of Midwifery*, 28(4): 210–11.

World Health Organization (WHO) (2018) *Intrapartum Care for a Positive Childbirth Experience*. Geneva: World Health Organization.

Case study 3
Martha: support or stigma?

Kelda Folliard and Kylie Burke

Introduction

This case study explores the role of the midwife in supporting women with mental health diagnoses during pregnancy. The decisions and dilemmas focus on providing continuity of care in the context of a complex situation where the client view and professional view about a course of action are not always the same. The case unfolds over several consultations reflecting the nature of midwifery care across the continuum of pregnancy.

Initial consultation

Martha attended her initial appointment with me when she was around nine weeks' pregnant. At first Martha appeared quite shy and struggled to make eye contact when I asked for the details of her medical and obstetric history. She told me this was her second pregnancy and that her older child, Maya, was in the reception year at school. I also had a reception-aged child, and we shared the challenges of helping them settle in at school. Martha's new partner, David, was at work so Martha attended the appointment alone.

VALUE: rapport building (Sully and Dallas, 2010)

As our conversation moved on to routine antenatal booking questions about Martha's personal, social and mental health history, she became increasingly uncomfortable about sharing information. Martha disclosed that her family had money worries and that she left school at 14, after which she lived with a foster family for a brief period. However, Martha did not offer any further details about this and due to her clear discomfort I did not press her further. She also disclosed that aged 17 she moved in with Maya's father, who was emotionally abusive, and that shortly afterwards she became pregnant. I told Martha

VALUE: empathy (Moudatsou et al, 2020)

that I was sorry she had experienced a challenging time growing up and in her relationships.

Martha informed me that she had received care from secondary mental health services in the past but was discharged two years ago. When asked why this was, Martha explained that she had received community psychiatric support for a month at the age of 20 following the breakdown of a violent relationship and her subsequent suicide attempt. She said this was when she first received a diagnosis of borderline personality disorder. Martha said she had tried various medications to help her mental health in the past, including anti-depressants and benzodiazepines. She also explained that for the past two years her mental health had been stable and when I offered a mental health referral she declined. Her responses to routine mental health screening questions indicated no immediate concerns (Whooley et al, 1997).

THEORY: assessing need and facilitating signposting or referral (NICE, 2014)

Martha told me her relationship with David was new, describing him as kind, and said they were both pleased about the pregnancy although it was unplanned. They were hoping for David to move into the house Martha shared with Maya in the coming weeks. She said money was tight, but she was managing and had no debt. When asked about other family or social support, Martha said she was estranged from her family and had a few friends, who were busy with their own young children. I suggested that I see Martha regularly during her pregnancy and offered a first baby schedule of antenatal care and delayed midwifery discharge, which she accepted.

THEORY: personalised care (NHS-E, 2019)

After the initial consultation

Reflections

I felt aware that there was much more to Martha's story. I was worried about whether I had missed any key information because I did not want to ask her lots of questions that may have been upsetting or alienated her early in our professional relationship. I was concerned that there may

EVIDENCE: reasons for non-disclosure in psychosocial midwifery assessment (Mule et al, 2022)

have been safeguarding issues that I had not fully understood as I could see Martha was vulnerable, but I found it
hard to get a sense of how stable things really were for her.
When Martha said she had borderline personality disorder
I was aware that I did not really understand this condition
and how it may affect her. I could see she had little social
support, which worried me because I know how important
support in pregnancy is, but I also thought this suited her
and that she did not want to be close to others. Plus,
Martha told me that her mental health was stable, so I think
it was important not to question this, but what if I was
missing something and had not really understood any
potential safeguarding risks?

EVIDENCE: social support is
protective against poor perinatal
mental health (Nakamura et al,
2020)

VALUE: trust (Sousa-Duarte
et al, 2020)

Actions

I decided to discuss Martha's history and care with
colleagues so I could be prepared for when we next met.
I spoke to the specialist mental health midwife about
different options for support. It was agreed that at present
there was nothing to indicate a mental health referral as
Martha reported stable mental health in the context of an
unplanned but wanted pregnancy, and within a supportive
relationship. However, it was clear that given Martha's history I should have a low threshold for making a perinatal
mental health team (PMHT) referral should there be any
change in Martha's mental state (Knight et al, 2021).
Martha had stated that she did not require any mental
health support at this time.

MODEL: access to specialist
perinatal mental healthcare
(RCM, 2018)

The specialist midwife explained that borderline personality disorder is understood to be grounded in trauma,
which seemed to fit with Martha's mention of her childhood
circumstances. She also explained that this diagnosis can
make people feel stigmatised since it implies a flawed personality rather than acknowledging the traumatic root
causes of the condition.

EVIDENCE: O'Carroll (2022)
suggested that labelling people
with personality disorder in
adulthood deflects away from the
potential association with events
in childhood associated with
trauma and poverty; political
economy theory and health
(McDonnell et al, 2009)

The specialist midwife also told me about other
organisations which could be of help to Martha, including
a perinatal mental health charity which supports people

MODEL: the role of the voluntary
community social enterprise in
mental health support (Coe and
Barlow, 2013)

who are isolated and experiencing poor mental health during pregnancy.

At a caseload meeting with the health visitor, I explained my concerns about Martha. We agreed that at Martha's next appointment I would offer a joint home visit with the health visitor to further explore any additional support needs she may have. This would also be an early opportunity for the health visitor to establish a relationship with Martha. I completed a 'cause for concern' form to make the safeguarding team aware of Martha's social and mental health history and vulnerabilities, and to highlight my plan for joint working with the health visitor, including further risk assessment.

MODEL: multi-professional
working; pre-birth risk
assessment (NSPCC, 2014)

Second consultation

Martha returned to see me for her 16-week antenatal appointment and was physically well. However, she was withdrawn, and when I gently asked her how things were, she broke down in tears. Martha explained that David had ended the relationship after some big arguments when she found evidence of his suspected infidelity. She said David no longer wanted to be involved with her and the baby. As Martha explained this, she became increasingly upset and fraught, saying that she felt panicked about how she would manage. I offered sympathy and explained that we would take as much time as needed to talk and understand her situation and to think about how best to support her.

VALUES: empathy and
compassion (Sully and Dallas,
2010)

THEORY: person-centred theory
(Rogers, 1961)

Martha explained that the arguments with David coincided with the anniversary of her mother's death from alcoholism and drug misuse when Martha was 19. Martha said that every year she finds the time around the anniversary overwhelming. She said her mood was extremely low and that she had previously taken anti-depressant medication, which had helped, but she felt anxious about doing so during pregnancy in case she harmed the baby (Hippman and Balneaves, 2018). Martha explained she had been experiencing poor sleep and intrusive thoughts about her mother's death. I advised Martha to talk to her general practitioner (GP) about medication, and I offered a referral

EVIDENCE: motherless mothers
(Rowe and Harman, 2014

to the perinatal mental health team, assuring her that any referrals would only be made with her involvement.

THEORY: trauma-informed care (Law et al, 2021)

Martha stated she did not want any referrals or to speak to the GP about medication. She expressed worry that people would think she is a bad mother if she asked for mental health support in pregnancy, and that Maya might be taken away from her. We agreed that our next contact would be a joint visit at home with her health visitor in the coming weeks.

MODEL: consent and capacity

VALUE: reluctance to seek mental health support due to stigma (Moore et al, 2017)

MODEL: multi-agency working

After the second consultation

Reflections

I felt genuinely concerned after Martha left the appointment because I thought she needed some mental health support since there was a deterioration in her mood, which was affecting her sleep and her thinking. I felt out of my depth when she started asking about medication use in pregnancy. I was conflicted because I knew I needed to maintain a trauma-informed approach to her care, maintaining Martha's choice and control, so any care that was planned needed to take this into account. Moreover, I thought that Martha's reluctance to accept help was because of worry about stigma, which I think might prevent pregnant women and birthing people asking for help when they need it.

THEORY: trauma-informed-care (Law et al, 2021)

EVIDENCE: stigma of poor perinatal mental health (RCOG, 2017)

On top of this I now understood more about the adverse childhood experiences which had made Martha vulnerable to poor mental health and life chances. I hoped that we might be able to revisit the possibility of seeking extra support at our next meeting.

THEORY: adverse childhood experiences (Asmundson and Afifi, 2020)

However, despite my understanding of Martha's personal challenges and the desire to maintain our relationship, I was concerned about whether there were safeguarding risks that I needed to act on. I was worried about whether Martha's poor mental health would affect her ability to parent and meet her children's needs. My professional responsibility to safeguard Martha's daughter and unborn baby meant I would potentially need to make a safeguarding referral, which was precisely the thing that scared Martha the most.

MODEL: professional responsibility (NMC, 2019), safeguarding duty of care (DfE, 2018)

Actions

I spoke to the GP about my concerns for Martha and to advise them that Martha's mood was low but that she was reluctant to commence medication or have any mental health support. I also spoke to the health visitor to agree a plan for a joint visit to Martha at home to complete a pre-birth risk assessment, enabling exploration of further support needs and level of vulnerability.

MODEL: pre-birth risk
assessment (NSPCC, 2014),
multi-agency working

The joint visit

I arranged a joint visit with the health visitor to see Martha at home, but unfortunately Martha cancelled the appointment twice. This raised concerns about her engagement, but on our third attempt to visit Martha she was at home and invited us into the house. Martha appeared upset, tense and struggled to make eye contact with either of us. She looked tired and unkempt; the house was warm and furnished but appeared chaotic with toys and clothes on the floor in the lounge and hallway.

Martha discussed attending her 20-week scan a few days beforehand, and said she went alone. She informed us that the scan was normal and that she had been told she was having a boy. She said she felt low and appeared ambivalent about her pregnancy, saying she did not really think about the baby at all. Martha said that David did not wish to be involved with her or the baby as he was in a new relationship.

EVIDENCE: bonding in pregnancy
and mental health (Rossen
et al, 2017)

When I asked questions to ascertain the impact of her mood, Martha spoke of persistent feelings of depression with increased thoughts of suicide. When probed about active plans or intent to end her life, Martha disclosed that she had increasingly been having thoughts about driving her car into the central reservation of the dual carriageway. Martha said she had not slept well for several weeks and felt constantly tired. She told us she felt detached from the baby and had no emotion or feelings of connection when seeing the scan.

EVIDENCE: screening for
depression (Whooley et al, 1997)

I asked Martha if she would consider seeing the GP about her mood and medication, as discussed at our previous appointment. Martha became tearful and angry, abruptly shouting that there was nothing wrong with her and that medication would not solve anything. Concerned about Martha's thoughts of harm to herself, I mentioned a referral to the Crisis Resolution and Home Treatment Team (CRHT) and Children's Services for additional support. At this point Martha became agitated; she shouted at us that she did not need or want any help from anyone, was not having a mental health crisis and that she wanted us to leave. As we left, I offered to call Martha later that day to see how she was feeling.

VALUE: trust

After the joint visit

Reflections

I felt sure I had made the right decision suggesting to Martha a referral to CHRT and Children's Services as it was evident her mental health and well-being had deteriorated. Despite this making her angry, I was concerned that without further support there was potentially the risk of harm to herself, Maya and the unborn baby. My professional responsibilities were to act in her best interests and joint working between agencies seemed the most appropriate pathway in this situation (NMC, 2018; NMC, 2019). I felt an open and honest approach was essential to my relationship with Martha. However, this felt like a difficult balancing act of being proactive and sensitive while remaining objective.

EVIDENCE: safeguarding children and supporting women (Humberstone, 2015)

Should I have tried to arrange another joint visit before considering referrals to mental health services and Children's Services, by exploring with the health visitor early help support (Local Government Association, 2017)? I had offered to refer Martha for mental health support two times previously, which she declined, but did I respond too quickly to her behaviour? I know that when people have had traumatic experiences, they can find it difficult to trust others so maybe we needed more time to build our relationship before she would accept help. Was Martha's presentation simply a response to her social stressors and her previous experiences of trauma?

EVIDENCE: trauma response (Maercker et al, 2022)

I felt disappointed that my relationship with Martha might have deteriorated. My intention was to ensure she received support, but instead had I made her less trusting by taking away the option of choice and maintaining control?

Actions

I returned to the health centre and spoke to the health visitor and GP. We recognised that Martha was demonstrating concerning behaviours that required escalation based on the following:

THEORY: red flags

- demonstration of perinatal red flags including active thoughts about ending her life, persistent feelings of estrangement from the unborn baby and a significant deterioration in mood;

- Martha had not arranged to see her GP to discuss feeling low in mood and starting anti-depressant medication;

- potential disengagement with healthcare professionals (midwife and health visitor).

The health visitor advised that she would contact Maya's school to discuss her attendance and enquire if the school had any concerns regarding Martha and Maya. Following discussion with the GP, it was decided that referrals to the Crisis Resolution and Home Treatment Team (CRHT) and Children's Services were needed due to Martha's current presentation and concerns around her ability to prioritise and safeguard Maya and the unborn baby without support.

MODEL: safeguarding children (DfE, 2018)

I called Martha and was pleased that she answered, especially after the events earlier that day. She said a friend had come to be with her as she had been so distressed. I informed Martha that I was concerned for her well-being and would make a referral to CRHT and Children's Services, stressing the importance of her receiving appropriate support. Martha accepted this.

MODEL: multi-agency working

I contacted Children's Services via telephone, expressing my concerns about Martha's well-being and perinatal mental health red flags. The case was referred to the local authority, who advised that a decision on whether the case would be opened by Children's Services would be made within one working day and that I would be informed of the outcome (DfE, 2018).

The next morning I received a call from the GP informing me that the CRHT had been in contact following their visit to Martha at home. A full mental health assessment had taken place and a follow-up plan formulated for Martha to commence anti-depressants with ongoing monitoring from the GP. Martha also accepted a referral to the peri-natal mental health team to support her to build a relation-ship with her unborn baby. I felt relieved that Martha had the appropriate structures in place to support her mental health during pregnancy and post birth.

Questions for reflection and discussion

1. Consider at which point it would have been most appropriate to make a referral to CRHT and Children's Services in relation to any safeguarding concerns and Martha's deteriorating mental health. What would you expect the outcome of those referrals to be?

2. What effect did the midwife's actions have on their professional relationship with Martha and how could they have managed this situation differently?

3. If the midwife had not made the mental health and safeguarding referrals, what might the implications have been for Martha, Maya and her unborn baby?

4. How could the midwife have helped Martha to be more accepting of an earlier referral for mental health support? Consider why this is important and what barriers might she have been facing.

5. What professional support is available in the workplace for midwives caring for women and birthing people with complex needs?

6. How can midwives ensure effective multi-agency working for women and birthing people with complex needs?

Helpful resources

BUMPS – https://medicinesinpregnancy.org

Marcé Society – https://marcesociety.com

Maternal Mental Health Alliance – https://maternalmentalhealthalliance.org

PANDAS – https://pandasfoundation.org.uk

Royal College of Psychiatrists – www.rcpsych.ac.uk

References

Asmundson, G and Afifi, T (2020) *Adverse Childhood Experiences: Using Evidence to Advance Research, Practice, Policy, and Prevention.* Cambridge, MA: Elsevier Academic Press.

Coe, C and Barlow, J (2013) Supporting Women with Perinatal Mental Health Problems: The Role of the Voluntary Sector. *Community Practitioner*, 86: 23–7.

Department for Education (DfE) (2018) *Working Together to Safeguard Children.* [online] Available at: https://assets.publishing.service.gov.uk/government/uploads/system/uploads/attachment_data/file/942454/Working_together_to_safeguard_children_inter_agency_guidance.pdf (accessed 9 March 2023).

Hippmann, C and Balneaves, L G (2018) Women's Decision Making about Antidepressant Use During Pregnancy: A Narrative Review. *Depression and Anxiety*, 35: 1158–67.

Humberstone, S (2015) Mental Illness in Pregnancy: Midwives Supporting Women and Safeguarding Babies. *The Practising Midwife*, 18: 18–20.

Knight, M, Bunch, K, Tuffnell, D, Patel, R, Shakespeare, J, Kotnis, R, Kenyon, S and Kurinczuk, J J (eds) (2021) *Saving Lives, Improving Mothers' Care: Lessons Learned to Inform Maternity Care from the UK and Ireland Confidential Enquiries into Maternal Deaths and Morbidity 2017–19.* Oxford: National Perinatal Epidemiology Unit, University of Oxford.

Law, C, Wolfenden, L, Sperlich, M and Taylor, J (2021) *A Good Practice Guide to Support Implementation of Trauma-Informed Care in the Perinatal Period.* [online] Available at: www.england.nhs.uk/wp-content/uploads/2021/02/BBS-TIC-V8.pdf (accessed 9 March 2023).

Local Government Association (2017) *Improving Outcomes for Children and Families in the Early Years: A Key Role for Health Visiting Services.* [online] Available at: www.local.gov.uk/sites/default/files/documents/improving-outcomes-childr-bf1.pdf (accessed 9 March 2023).

Maercker, A, Cloitre, M, Bachem, R, Schlumpf, Y R, Khoury, B, Hitchcock, C and Bohus, M (2022) Complex Post-Traumatic Stress Disorder. *The Lancet*, 400: 60–72.

McDonnell, O, Lohan, M, Hyde, A and Porter, S (2009) *Social Theory, Health and Healthcare.* Basingstoke: Palgrave Macmillan.

Moore, D, Drey, N and Ayers, S (2017) Use of Online Forums for Perinatal Mental Illness, Stigma, and Disclosure: An Exploratory Model. *JMIR Mental Health*, 20(4).

Moudatsou, M, Stavropoulou, A, Philalithis, A and Koukouli, S (2020) The Role of Empathy in Health and Social Care Professionals. *Healthcare (Basel)*, 8(1): 26.

Mule, V, Reilly, N M, Schmied, V, Kingston, D and Austin, M P V (2022) Why Do Some Pregnant Women Not Fully Disclose at Comprehensive Psychosocial Assessment with Their Midwife? *Women and Birth*, 35: 80–6.

Nakamura, A, Suter-Dalley, A L, El-Khoury, L F, Thierry, X, Gressier, F, Melchior, M and van der Waerden, J (2020) Informal and Formal Social Support During Pregnancy and Joint Maternal and Paternal Postnatal Depression: Data from the French Representative ELFE Cohort Study. *International Journal of Social Psychiatry*, 66: 431–41.

National Institute for Health and Care Excellence (NICE) (2014) *Antenatal and Postnatal Mental Health: Clinical Management and Service Guidance.* [online] Available at: www.nice.org.uk/guidance/cg192/resources/antenatal-and-postnatal-mental-health-clinical-management-and-service-guidance-pdf-35109869806789 (accessed 9 March 2023).

NHS-E (2019) *Universal Personalised Care: Implementing the Comprehensive Model.* [online] Available at: www.england.nhs.uk/publication/universal-personalised-care-implementing-the-comprehensive-model (accessed 9 March 2023).

NSPCC (2014) *Risk Assessment Pre-Birth: A Practice Model.* [online] Available at: https://spi.web.ox.ac.uk/files/pre-birth-assessment (accessed 9 March 2023).

Nursing & Midwifery Council (NMC) (2018) *The Code: Professional Standards of Practice and Behaviour for Nurses, Midwives and Nursing Associates.* London: Nursing & Midwifery Council.

Nursing & Midwifery Council (NMC) (2019) *Standards of Proficiency for Midwives.* [online] Available at: www.nmc.org.uk/globalassets/sitedocuments/standards/standards-of-proficiency-for-midwives.pdf (accessed 23 January 2023)

O'Carroll, A (2022) *The Triple F**k Syndrome: How Medicine Contributes to the Systematic Oppression of People Born into Poverty.* BJGP Life. [online] Available at: https://bjgplife.com/the-triple-fk-syndrome-how-medicine-contributes-to-the-systemic-oppression-of-people-born-into-poverty (accessed 9 March 2023).

Rogers, C R (1961) *On Becoming a Person: A Therapist's View of Psychotherapy.* Boston, MA: Houghton Mifflin.

Rossen, L, Hutchinson, D, Wilson, J, Burns, L, Allsop, S, Elliott, E J, Jacobs, S, Macdonald, J A, Olsson, C and Mattick, R P (2017) Maternal Bonding through Pregnancy and Postnatal: Findings from an Australian Longitudinal Study. *American Journal of Perinatology*, 34(8): 808–17.

Rowe, B and Harman, B A (2014) Motherless Mothers: Maternally Bereaved Women in Their Everyday Roles as Mothers. *Journal of Family Studies*, 20(1): 28–38.

Royal College of Midwives (RCM) (2018) *Specialist Mental Health Midwives: What They Do and Why They Matter*. [online] Available at: www.rcm.org.uk/media/2370/specialist-mental-health-midwives-what-they-do-and-why-they-matter.pdf (accessed 9 March 2023).

Royal College of Obstetricians and Gynaecologists (RCOG) (2017) *Maternal Mental Health: Women's Voices*. [online] Available at: www.rcog.org.uk/media/3ijbpfvi/maternal-mental-health-womens-voices.pdf (accessed 9 March 2023).

Sousa-Duarte, F, Brown, P and Mendes, A M (2020) Healthcare Professionals' Trust in Patients: A Review of the Theoretical and Empirical Literatures. *Sociology Compass*, 14(10): 1–15.

Sully, P and Dallas, J (2010) *Essential Communication Skills for Nursing and Midwifery*. 2nd ed. London: Elsevier.

Whooley, M A, Avins, A L, Miranda, J and Browner, W S (1997) Case-Finding Instruments for Depression: Two Questions Are as Good as Many. *Journal of General Internal Medicine*, 12(7): 439–45.

Part 2

Prioritising care

Case study 4
Baby Alex: doing the right thing

Kirsty Tweedie and Jo Knox

Introduction

This case study explores the challenges midwives may face when managing conflicts of opinion, where a less experienced midwife neonatal examiner (MNE) identifies an anomaly when undertaking the newborn and infant physical examination (NIPE) and feels that they need to escalate even when these concerns are not supported by their colleague. Focusing on the contribution of theory and knowledge to the development of competent perform-ance shows how even inexperienced practitioners need to develop the confidence and courage to ensure that the best care provision is provided. In addition, they must be supported and encouraged to ensure that the care of women and their families is central to their practice. The case study closes with ideas for further actions to develop reflective skills, together with suggestions for evidence-based enquiry and supportive exploration with colleagues.

Newborn and infant physical examination

The NHS newborn and infant physical examination (NIPE) screening programme's main aims are to:

- *identify and refer all children born with congenital abnormalities of the eyes, heart, hips and (in males) testes, where these are detectable, within 72 hours of birth to further identify those abnormalities that may become detectable by 6 to 8 weeks of age, at the infant phys-ical examination*

- *reduce morbidity and mortality*

The NIPE programme screens babies (ideally) within 72 hours of birth (NIPE newborn screening examination) and again at 6 to 8 weeks of age (NIPE infant examination) for conditions relating to the: eyes, heart, hips, testes (if applicable) (United Kingdom National Screening Committee (UKNSC), 2021)

These ages are recommended based on the best practice and current evidence and should facili-tate a prompt referral for early clinical assessment.

Table 4.1 Newborn and infant physical examination

Baby Alex is examined

Baby Alex is 36 hours old and was born at 39 weeks by emergency caesarean section; he had been transferred to the ward with his mother, where she was receiving post-operative care. I was the midwife responsible for the care of Alex and his mother while on the ward. The routine care included a NIPE for Alex within the first 72 hours of birth (UKNSC, 2021; see Table 4.1). I am an experienced midwife and recently qualified as an MNE. I introduced myself: *'My name is Jamie, I would like to undertake the newborn and infant physical examination, which is part of the newborn screening programme in the UK. Were you given information about this at one of your recent appointments with the midwife? I will explain everything as I go along, and you can ask me to stop at any point if you don't understand or would like more information about any aspect of the examination.'* I handed Alex's mother a leaflet containing all the information pertinent to the examination and advised both of Alex's parents of the limitations of the examination and advised them that a repeat of the NIPE would be performed by the GP as part of the six–eight-week appointment. Having given them some time to peruse the leaflet, I answered their questions, and they gave me verbal consent to proceed with the examination. Prior to commencing the examination, I reviewed the maternal antenatal, intrapartum obstetric and midwifery records, and the baby's records. I also took a detailed history from Alex's parents and advised them of the expected feeding pattern and neonatal behaviour. Alex should be fed on demand so normally we would expect him to have six to eight feeds in a 24-hour period. I asked Alex's parent's a few questions in order to identify any red flags:

- *'Have you noticed Alex becoming breathless or showing any change in his skin colour, for example becoming paler at rest or when he feeds?'*

- *'Do you have any concerns with his feeding or behaviour?'*

- *'Has Alex appeared too tired to feed, or have you felt that he has been particularly quiet or lethargic?'*

In order to assess whether there were any concerns with regard to Alex's tone, I asked his parents if he appeared to be floppy at any point. Alex's parents said that they had no concerns regarding his feeding or his behaviour, and therefore no red flags were apparent.

I considered other potential red flags associated with cardiac anomalies and rechecked with Alex's parents following the examination and prior to escalation to my medical colleagues to ensure that I was able to provide a full and detailed referral via the use of the SBAR tool.

> *EVIDENCE: Tappero and Honeyfield (2019) describe other clinical red flags for coronary heart disease as follows: breathlessness, poor feeding/inadequate weight gain, sweating, colour change, lower limb saturations <95%, absent/weak femoral pulses, precordium, apex beat, hepatomegaly, heart murmurs*

On review of the maternal antenatal records, I noted that Alex's mother was diagnosed as having epilepsy in childhood and had been prescribed the anti-epileptic drug (AED) carbamazepine for this. I asked her about this and whether she had spoken to a healthcare professional about the medication she took for the epilepsy.

'Oh, I didn't go to the doctor cos I was afraid they'd change my tablets. My epilepsy used to be so bad, and I would have fits when I was in stressful situations, but it has been okay for such a long time, maybe two or three years. I know you're supposed to ask the doctor if you are thinking about having a baby, but it happened really quickly. So, I just thought, it'll be okay, I'm pregnant now and I don't want to have to mess around with new tablets that might make everything worse. So, I just left it. The community midwife did say something about epilepsy meds, but I didn't want to hear, really… does that sound bad? Do you think I've caused a problem? Is it my fault if there's something wrong with his him, like his heart?'

> *EVIDENCE: ensure women with epilepsy (particularly if they are taking anti-epileptic drug (AED) treatment) receive pre-pregnancy counselling (NICE, 2022). The Royal College of Obstetricians and Gynaecologists' (RCOG, 2016) Green-top Guideline 68 recommends that exposure to sodium valproate and other anti-epileptic drugs should be minimised by changing the medication prior to conception.*

The cardiovascular aspect of the NIPE examination includes observation of the external chest and palpation of the precordium to rule out anomalies such as heaves or thrills. Heart rate and rhythm are assessed as well as auscultation of the heart sounds. Documentation of normal heart sounds would be documented as S1 + S2 + 0, which represents the presence of two normal heart sounds and no additional heart sounds. S1 is created by the closure of the mitral and tricuspid valves at the beginning of ventricular contraction, while S2 is created by the closure of the aortic and the pulmonic valves at the end of ventricular systole and the beginning of ventricular diastole (Tappero and Honeyfield, 2019). During the auscultation of Alex's heart sounds, I noted two normal heart sounds plus a third heart sound, which I described to Alex's parents as a murmur. Heart murmurs are usually due to vibrations in the blood stream within the great vessels and the surrounding vessels of the heart as a result of turbulent flow. Murmurs can be defined using the Levine scale which moves through six grades from grade 1, which represents the lowest intensity, to grade 6, which represents the loudest intensity and is often associated with a palpable thrill (Tappero and Honeyfield, 2019). In Alex's case I noted a low intensity murmur with no palpable heaves or thrills and a Levine grade of 2. Due to the timeliness of the cardiovascular adaptations occurring at birth it is possible that a third heart sound may be identifiable and this is associated with an incomplete cardiovascular adaptation such as a patent ductus arteriosus which has not had adequate time for complete closure after birth.

VALUE: professional boundaries

THEORY: expertise (Benner, 1984)

Having completed a careful examination of the cardiovascular system I believe I heard a third heart sound; this was in the form of a diastolic murmur. With careful consideration to ensure that the way I communicated my findings to Alex's parents was both sensitive and clear, I maintained eye contact with them and said '*I have listened to Alex's heart. I can hear the normal sounds of lub and dub and the rhythm and rate both also appear to be normal; however, I believe I can hear a third heart sound. When a baby is born, the way the blood circulates around the body changes and this third heart sound that I think I can hear could relate to those changes. Despite being an experienced midwife, I am still reasonably inexperienced as a neonatal examiner and for that reason I will ask for another opinion from a more experienced colleague to see if they agree with my findings. Do you have any questions for me at this point?*' Alex's mother asked: '*Could this be to do with the anti-epileptic medication I have been taking?*' I replied: '*It is impossible to attribute something like this to any one thing. However, it is recommended that if you are taking medicines for epilepsy that you have a review with your doctors prior to trying for a baby to ensure that your medication is safe during pregnancy. This would be my advice if you plan to have another baby in the future but in terms of what I can hear with Alex's heart it is impossible to say.'*

Due to my inexperience as a midwife newborn examiner (MNE) I sought confirmation of my findings by way of a second opinion from a more experienced MNE. I advised Alex's parents of my findings and that, due to me being a novice MNE and the potential for there to be a murmur as a result of the potential of incomplete cardiovascular changes occurring after birth, I would be seeking a second opinion from a more experienced MNE. My senior colleague reported that she did not hear a third heart sound and advised myself and Alex's parents that she felt that the heart sounds were in fact normal. I was still concerned as I was quite sure of my findings, and I informed Alex's parents that I would escalate for a further review from the neonatologist. I am sure of my findings and have the courage, commitment and competence to further escalate.

VALUE: duty of candour

Although the senior MNE had informed Alex's parents that she didn't suspect an anomaly, there is potential to miss this anomaly.

I escalated to the neonatologist using the SBAR tool. This is a nationally recognised and effective communication tool used in healthcare settings to provide a comprehensive handover. Following the neonatologist's full cardiovascular examination, it was concluded that a third heart sound was detectable. This was reassuring for me as it confirmed my findings and enhanced my confidence with regard to my skills as an MNE. It was also reassuring that I felt able to apply the evidence to my practice in terms of being able to attribute the use of carbamazepine to my findings.

MODEL: communication. Situation, Background, Assessment, Recommendation (SBAR) communication tool (NHS England and NHS Improvement, 2021)

THEORY: expert practice. I felt confident and able in terms of my NIPE examination skills

VALUE: professional boundaries – aware of own limitations and the appropriateness of referral for additional opinions

Careful consideration was paid to how the findings were relayed to Alex's parents and their association with the use of carbamazepine. Advanced communication skills were used to ensure the avoidance of attributing blame or guilt. This is important particularly since it is not possible to be able to directly associate the use of carbamazepine with a structural cardiac anomaly during pregnancy, and nor was it confirmed that a structural anomaly was present at this stage.

MODEL: communication

Communicating with the parents to inform them of my findings, using communication skills to address the need for senior opinion and further communication to escalate for a medical opinion based on my confidence in my examination. Breaking bad news is a sensitive and complex task which requires practice and a considered tactful approach. I structured how I broke the news to the parents using the SPIKES model. Using a model such as SPIKES (S – Setting; P – Perception; I – Invitation or Information; K – Knowledge; E – Empathy; S – Strategy and summary) provides clarity and structure and aids breaking bad news.

Reflections

As an expert midwife but newly qualified MNE I was confident in my commitment and courage to seek additional help and advice where my examination of the heart sounds was concerned. What I feel I did lack was the experience and expertise to have complete conviction in my clinical judgement. On finding the cardiac anomaly, I felt it was within my professional remit to refer on to confirm my findings due to my lack of experience in this skill. I therefore sought the advice from a more experienced senior MNE who disagreed with my findings. This then made me consider my own abilities and my lack of experience in cardiac auscultation skills but my experience as a healthcare practitioner led me to seek further advice by way of escalating my concern to a more senior MNE colleague. This demonstrated my courage, conviction and commitment to recognise my professional boundaries, my limited experience in undertaking NIPE examinations and ensured that I was delivering a gold standard of care with the patient being central to that.

Due to this being my first time recognising abnormal heart sounds outside of a simulated experience, I did doubt myself and felt that my experience was limited and that this may impact on the accuracy of my findings. This prompted me to seek further advice and affirmation of my clinical judgement. This was slightly challenging for me as I am an experienced midwife, but I found myself in a situation where I was the novice and not the expert. As an experienced healthcare practitioner, I did feel comfortable explaining my findings to the parents, but I also had to explain to them that I am not experienced in this clinical skill and would therefore feel the need to refer to a more experienced senior NME colleague to confirm my findings. Due to the potential of causing undue alarm, I used compassionate communication skills to relay this information to them. I feel that it is important to impart information in an honest, accurate but compassionate way. This was not compromising for me as I am aware of my professional boundaries and limitations (the Code, NMC, 2018a). When the more experienced senior NME contradicted my findings, I found this to be difficult because I still felt a level of conviction that my findings were accurate and this caused a professional compromise for me in that I felt unable to completely accept the findings of my colleague despite her experience and expertise. Hence, I felt the need to escalate to a medical colleague for further opinion. I did this in a professional and clinically sound manner by using a recognised communication tool (SBAR). Having to escalate to a medical colleague made me feel uncomfortable because I do respect my senior NME colleagues. But I must have the courage to be sure of my own competence and clinical judgement despite my lack of experience and am committed to delivering excellent and safe patient-centred care.

THEORY: novice to expert (Benner, 1984)

MODEL: Baile et al (2000)

Actions

I demonstrated commitment to up-to-date evidence-based practice; the UKNSC underpins the standards and requirements regarding the NIPE. This is the evidence base used to underpin the practitioner's knowledge and expert skills and monitor quality assurance in relation to performing the NIPE in practice. The evidence upholds the need to refer on and escalate where clinical anomalies are suspected. I recognised my own inexperience in relation to performing the NIPE and as evidence would support, I escalated my concern to a more experienced colleague. This also upholds the Code (NMC, 2018a).

Part of compassionate communication includes connecting the feelings of parents with the potential impact of clinical findings while maintaining honesty and clarity. I acknowledged that being unsure of my findings may cause distress. In order to maintain my professional responsibility and to ensure that I was providing patient-centred care, I recognised that providing honest and clear information was imperative. I achieved this by avoiding terminology that may have been difficult for Alex's parents to understand. I maintained eye contact with the parents, allowing time for them to respond and question, and was careful to avoid the perception of apportioning blame. I was also careful to ensure that Alex's parents understood that this was a clinical suspicion and not a diagnosis.

Despite being a qualified healthcare professional for some time, I felt confident that I had auscultated a third heart sound. However, due to my inexperience in this clinical skill, I felt the need for a second opinion to ensure I was providing safe patient care. I showed professionalism in that I was delivering care which was within my sphere of practice (the Code, NMC, 2018a). However, I also demonstrated humility and honesty by acknowledging my clinical limitations due to my inexperience. I demonstrated courage and commitment to ensuring that I provided safe patient-centred care by requesting a second opinion from a more experienced NIPE practitioner.

I escalated to a medical colleague when the findings of the more experienced MNE contradicted mine. I displayed professional competence, courage and patient-centred care when I escalated my concern to my medical colleague. Part of being a professional involves effective and considerate communication within a professional environment which can be fraught with difficulty when there is conflict of opinion. It is important that healthcare practitioners can demonstrate both compassionate communication to people within their care but also to other professional colleagues. I was in a difficult position in that despite seeking reassurance in relation to my findings from a more experienced NIPE practitioner, I did not agree with her findings. In order to maintain excellent and safe patient care, I chose to escalate my findings to a medical colleague for a third opinion. The ability to be able to have both the courage and professional qualities needed to be able to manage a situation such as this where discomfort and upset may occur requires a complex and advanced ability to communicate.

Having the knowledge and understanding of the evidence attributed to advanced communication skills are essential. This was evident in the way that I managed the complexities of this situation. Having reviewed the maternal and antenatal and intrapartum notes, I noted the history of maternal epilepsy for which the mother was medicated.

> *EVIDENCE: heart defect – NIPE (Tappero and Honeyfield, 2019) suggest that some anti-epileptic drugs (AED) are a known associated risk factor for congenital heart disease (CHD). However, there are other associated factors, including: siblings with CHD, maternal diabetes mellitus, dysmorphic syndromes and structural malformations, and excess maternal alcohol intake*

Questions for reflection and discussion

1. Consider the impact of lack of experience in performing a clinical skill and how this might affect overall confidence, taking account of how you would manage your own emotions.

2. Consider how the experienced healthcare practitioner might feel and act in a situation where they have had to revert from expert to novice.

3. Explore how Jamie demonstrated his commitment to duty of candour in this scenario.

4. Consider how the parents might feel in response to how you communicate your findings and the impact of the referral and escalation.

5. How might you manage the professional relationship between yourself and the experienced senior MNE that did not agree with your findings?

6. It is clear that you could be offended by a colleague disagreeing with your clinical findings. With this in mind, consider and discuss how you might go about seeking other opinions where there is already a conflict of ideas.

Helpful resources

Newborn and Infant Physical Examination (NIPE) Screening: Programme Overview – www.gov.uk/guidance/newborn-and-infant-physical-examination-screening-programme-overview

Newborn and Infant Physical Examination Screening Pathway Requirements Specification – www.gov.uk/government/publications/newborn-and-infant-physical-examination-screening-pathway-requirements-specification/newborn-and-infant-physical-examination-screening-pathway-requirements-specification

Newborn Screening Programme: Congenital Heart Disease – https://view-health-screening-recommendations.service.gov.uk/congenital-heart-disease

NHS Public Health Functions Agreement 2019–20, Service Specification No. 21, NHS Newborn and Infant Physical Examination Screening Programme – www.england.nhs.uk/wp-content/uploads/2017/04/Service-Specification-No.21-NIPE.pdf

The 6Cs – A Set of Values for All Health and Social Care Staff – www.england.nhs.uk/6cs/wp-content/uploads/sites/25/2015/03/introducing-the-6cs.pdf

References

Baile, W F, Buckman, R, Lenzi, R, Glober, G, Beale, E A and Kudelka, A P (2000) SPIKES – A Six-Step Protocol for Delivering Bad News: Application to the Patient with Cancer. *Oncologist*, 5(4): 302–11.

Benner, P (1984) *From Novice to Expert: Excellence and Power in Clinical Nursing Practice.* Boston, MA: Addison-Wesley Publishing Company (Pearson).

National Institute for Health and Care Excellence (NICE) (2022b) Epilepsies in Children, Young People and Adults. [online] Available at: www.nice.org.uk/guidance/ng217/resources/epilepsies-in-children-young-people-and-adults-pdf-66143780239813 (accessed 9 March 2023).

NHS England (2021) *Personalised Care and Support: Planning Guidance for Local Maternity Systems.* [online] Available at: www.england.nhs.uk/wp-content/uploads/2021/03/B0423-personalised-care-and-support-planning-guidance-for-lms.pdf (accessed 31 March 2023).

NHS England and NHS Improvement (2021) *SBAR Communication Tool: Situation, Background, Assessment, Recommendation.* [online] Available at: www.england.nhs.uk/wp-content/uploads/2021/03/qsir-sbar-communication-tool.pdf (accessed 9 March 2023).

Nursing & Midwifery Council (NMC) (2018a) *The Code: Professional Standards of Practice and Behaviour for Nurses, Midwives and Nursing Associates.* London: Nursing & Midwifery Council.

Nursing & Midwifery Council (NMC) (2018b) *Standards for Student Supervision and Assessment.* London: Nursing & Midwifery Council.

Royal College of Obstetricians and Gynaecologists (RCOG) (2016) *Epilepsy in Pregnancy.* Green-top Guideline No. 68. [online] Available at: www.rcog.org.uk/guidance/browse-all-guidance/green-top-guidelines/epilepsy-in-pregnancy-green-top-guideline-no-68 (accessed 9 March 2023).

Tappero, M and Honeyfield, E (2019) *Physical Assessment of the Newborn: A Comprehensive Approach to the Art of Physical Examination.* 6th ed. New York: Springer.

UK National Screening Committee (UKNSC) (2021) *Newborn and Infant Physical Examination (NIPE) Screening Programme Handbook,* updated 28 April 2021. Public Health England. [online] Available at: www.gov.uk/government/publications/newborn-and-infant-physical-examination-programme-handbook/newborn-and-infant-physical-examination-screening-programme-handbook (accessed 9 March 2023).

Case study 5
Molly and Sandra: novice and expert

Nicky Hadlett and Ruth Sanders

Introduction

The focus of this case study is on communication between an experienced practice supervisor and a first-year student midwife, and their interaction during intrapartum care with a couple wishing for a natural birth experience. The potential impact of communication on key players' feelings is captured by the words of Maya Angelou: *'I've learned that people will forget what you said, people will forget what you did, but people will never forget how you made them feel.'* The lasting impact of communication on individuals is explored primarily through the practice supervisor's perspective with an insightful consideration given to the student experience. The case study closes with ideas for further actions to develop understanding, and suggestions for personal reflection and exploration with colleagues.

Night shift on delivery suite

Sandra's view

19:30:

I have been allocated a student for tonight's night shift, Molly, a first-year midwifery student, and we are caring for a couple on the delivery suite. Molly has not worked here before and so I have oriented her to the area and made sure she knows to ask questions if she is unsure about anything. The couple, Birgitta and Jacques, strongly wish for no interventions and as natural as possible a birth experience.

MODEL: coaching

VALUES: compassion, family-centred choice

01:30:

Birgitta has been involuntarily pushing during the active second stage of her labour for the last 90 minutes and progress has been slow with few external signs visible and little descent confirmed on abdominal palpation.

EVIDENCE: NICE (2017). (See Note 1 at the end of this chapter)

EVIDENCE: NICE guidance, safety

The obstetric team is called and following assessment Birgitta is advised that the baby is extremely low in the

VALUE: collaborative practice. (See Note 2)

pelvis and will need some assistance in being born with forceps.

01:52:

Birgitta's baby is born with the use of forceps managed by the senior registrar. I encourage Molly to watch closely during this learning opportunity, which is her first experience of an assisted birth. At the beginning of the shift, we had discussed Molly's previous experiences, which had included administration of intramuscular injections. To consolidate Molly's previous experience, I directly supervise Molly to administer an intramuscular oxytocic immediately following the birth of the baby.

02:01:

The senior registrar delivers the placenta and places it in a receptacle on the delivery trolley. The senior registrar completes his notes on the computer and then leaves the room. I ask Molly to take a set of maternal observations following birth, which are all within normal parameters.

02:15:

I check the fundus and notice that it is not as well contracted as it was immediately after the placenta delivered. I then check the perineum and notice a brisk blood loss and Birgitta is starting to appear unwell. At this point Molly is engrossed in talking to Birgitta about options and choices they have for the placenta, and whether they would like to take it home to plant or encapsulate. I ask her to stop her conversation to come and assist me as I needed help to manage what I suspected was a post-partum haemorrhage.

Molly glared at me, not registering the tone of my voice or the urgency of the situation.

Molly's view

I was allocated to a new practice supervisor for a night shift on delivery suite where I had never worked before. We were looking after a lovely couple who were keen to have no intervention. However, due to a delay in the second

THEORY: novice to expert

MODELS: Standards for Student Supervision and Assessment (SSSA) (NMC, 2018b), exposure to new learning

THEORIES: consolidation of learning, development of clinical skills

MODEL: student-centred learning (Hamilton et al, 2020)

THEORIES: learning by theory and experience, learning by doing (Gibbs, 1988)

EVIDENCE: NICE (2017) CG190; RCOG (2016) Prevention and management of post-partum haemorrhage

VALUES: interprofessional communication, recognition of increased risk/additional needs

THEORY: working within the Code (NMC, 2018a)

MODEL: novice to expert

MODEL: use of modified early obstetric warning scores (MEOWS) (RCA, 2018)

VALUE: family-centred care

THEORIES: expert and novice roles, threshold concepts, coaching

EVIDENCE: RCOG (2016) Prevention and management of post-partum haemorrhage; NICE (2017). (See Note 3)

VALUE: communicating in an emergency

THEORY: NMC (2019)

EVIDENCE: Ockenden (2022)

stage of labour, Birgitta needed a birth assisted by forceps. This was my first experience of an assisted birth, and I felt overwhelmed by the sudden change from midwifery-led to obstetrician-led care.

I felt very saddened that Birgitta and Jacques did not have the birth experience they were hoping for. I tried to make this better for them by focusing on other positive activities that may improve their birth experience. I supported them to initiate breastfeeding and began to talk about options they could consider for their placenta.

While I was concentrating on communicating these options to Birgitta and Jacques, the practice supervisor, Sandra, spoke to me in a loud voice, interrupting me and insisting that I stop talking to the couple and go and help her. To me, this felt unprofessional and harsh, which upset me and made me feel embarrassed that this had happened in front of Birgitta and Jacques. It was as though she did not realise she was shouting and did not care about the woman's experiences or physiological birth processes. This made me feel that she was not a suitable midwife to be a practice supervisor because I was left feeling upset and unsupported on a labour ward where I have never been placed before.

Molly's reflections

Reflecting on this situation two days later, I am still upset and shocked that my practice supervisor did not really consider how important Birgitta and Jacques' birth experience was to them, and the actions that could have improved their experience. I have been talking to my student peers and have decided to report this to my programme lead at the university.

Sandra's reflections

As soon as I noticed that Birgitta was starting to look unwell, I tried to indicate this to Molly by changing my tone of voice and the urgency with which I spoke to her. Molly was so engrossed in talking to Birgitta and Jacques that

VALUE: developing new learning relationships

THEORY: 6Cs – Courage

MODEL: interprofessional working

EVIDENCE: recognition of a need for escalation to additional care needs (Ockenden, 2022)

THEORY: Better Births (NHS England, 2016), Birth Trauma Association

VALUES: empathy, mental health for student learners, student support services university well-being, counselling services

EVIDENCE: UNICEF, Baby Friendly Initiative standards

THEORY: Re:birth (RCM, 2022). (See Note 4)

VALUE: professional communication

EVIDENCE: Re:birth (oxytocin impacts on birth environment)

VALUE: reflection in practice about communication and impact of language on the actions of others

MODELS: NMC (2018b), responsibilities of practice supervisor

MODELS: university process for reporting a concern in practice, support for students encountering disturbing situations in practice; NMC SSSA (NMC, 2018b). (See Note 5)

MODEL: communication

she was entirely unaware of Birgitta's deterioration. Birgitta was starting to bleed heavily; she was cold, clammy and pale, unable to respond coherently to my questions. I estimated her MEOWS to be 4–5. Molly appeared to detach herself from the situation, becoming quiet and monosyllabic in her verbal communication. Her facial expression suggested that she was unhappy with the situation. My focus quickly shifted from the student to managing the unfolding emergency. I pulled the emergency bell and the labour suite co-ordinator, a second midwife and the senior registrar came to assist me. Once the situation was under control, I was aware that Molly was standing quietly in the background.

EVIDENCE: modified early obstetric warning scores – MBRRACE/RCOG

MODEL: Practical Obstetric Multi-Professional Training (PROMPT) model (2017)

Sandra's proposed actions

I was aware that Molly had been affected by the situation. I planned to speak to her once the couple were settled and stable to ascertain her understanding of the emergency and to ensure she knew why I had taken the steps that I had and communicated in such an urgent manner. I was unhappy that I was unable to have this conversation with Molly before the end of the shift because as soon as we had transferred Birgitta and Jacques to the postnatal ward, we were immediately allocated another woman in advanced labour.

THEORIES: professional communication and learner feedback

EVIDENCE: the Code (NMC, 2018a), Standard 8.2; NMC (2018b) SSSA, Standard 3.3

EVIDENCE: NMC SSSA

Having reflected on this situation on my way home from the shift, I feel the need to discuss with Molly's practice assessor her communication skills and appreciation of an unfolding emergency. I acknowledge that she is a first-year student and may not have experienced situations like this before; therefore, this is a valuable opportunity for her to develop her understanding.

MODEL: novice to expert, university curriculum content for Year 1

While I appreciate Molly is a first-year student with limited experience, I have considered directing her to study resources that may help her develop her understanding. I would also direct Molly to use her Collaborative Learning in Practice (CLiP) time to help her apply theory to the practice setting. I plan to seek Molly out when she is next on

EVIDENCE: NICE intrapartum guidance, RCOG massive obstetric haemorrhage, CLiP references, SBAR tools, communication skills, evidence-based practice shift and explore her emotional well-being with her to see if she needs to debrief this situation with me.

Debriefing following the care episode

Sandra's view

I was shocked to be approached by the student's programme lead, who wished to meet with myself and the student to explore the student's perception of this placement experience. In preparation for this meeting, I reflected on the student involvement during this care episode which escalated outside usual parameters. Reflecting has made me consider that the student could have been more upset than I had originally believed. As an experienced midwife and practice supervisor, I am confident that my practice is always safe, competent and caring towards the students I supervise. I have never received any negative communication from students about how I approach my practice supervisor role.

MODELS: Collaborative Learning in Practice (CLiP), emergency communications

VALUE: 6Cs – care, compassion

THEORIES: student well-being, staff debriefing

VALUES: professional experience, tacit knowledge

Molly's view

I was very nervous at being asked to meet with my programme lead and practice supervisor. I was scared I may have done something wrong and I would be asked to leave the course. I spoke to a friend in my cohort, who suggested I talk to my personal tutor. I explained to my personal tutor that I always use polite language and try and apply the NMC Code to my clinical learning experience. I was reassured by my personal tutor's advice to attend the meeting with an open mind and use all opportunities as learning and development experiences.

EVIDENCE: NMC (2018a)

VALUE: learning culture

Sandra's reflections

On reflection, having been an experienced midwife for a long time, I may not have related appropriately to the student's position at the novice end of the novice-to-expert trajectory. It is my duty as practice supervisor to be

THEORY: novice to expert

VALUE: *practising objectively*

EVIDENCE: *the Code (NMC, 2018a)*

MODEL: *educational audit*

EVIDENCE: *NMC (2018c), Part 1: Standards framework for nursing and midwifery education, NMC (2018b), Part 2: SSSA*

VALUE: *cross-boundary working*

EVIDENCE: *caring for the carers evidence, RCM (2022)*

objective and consider the student's perspective in the planning, delivery and evaluation of care. I need to remember that my primary concern is public safety and educating student midwives to uphold the NMC Code and the safety of those in their care. I need to be confident I am demonstrating appropriate role modelling to promote high-quality and safe student learning.

In my practice supervisor role, I need to have oversight of a student's knowledge, experience and well-being and their ability to apply theoretical knowledge to practice experiences. I feel disappointed that the student did not approach me to discuss and debrief the care episode but instead pursued another route to debrief.

It is part of my role to ensure that the student is offered and can access the right support at the right time in relation to any difficult clinical experiences. On reflection, I understand that it is imperative that I engage with academic staff so that students do not feel a divide between the placement and academic learning environments.

I have formulated a plan of action for future student learning experiences. To value and support student learning, considering students are the midwives of the future, I plan to:

• understand the complexity of the student's actions/ feelings;

• explore my actions and feelings related to supervising students in care episodes with which they are unfamiliar;

• develop a plan of how to support the student in their understanding of the situation while being sensitive to their level of learning and experience;

• help the student to understand actions I may take as a practice supervisor.

Further information

Note 1: the CG190 NICE guidance recommends that labour progress should be monitored in a range of ways, including observing the labouring woman's behaviour and assessing the effectiveness of pushing efforts and well-being of the baby. The fetal position should be considered, as should the onset of the second stage, and it may be deemed necessary to liaise with the obstetric team if care needs to change from midwifery-led to obstetric-led care (NICE, 2017).

Note 2: Lindqvist et al (2017, p 1) suggest that: *'The collaborative process is underpinned by a culture where everyone's contribution is valued. Collaborative practice empowers staff to embrace change and engage with innovation'*. The interaction between the obstetric and midwifery teams would give optimum person-centred care if Lindqvist et al's principles and values were to be followed.

Note 3: the National Institute for Health and Care Excellence (NICE, 2017) CG190 states that women and their birth companion should have a healthcare team member present to support and explain the unfolding emergency situation and respond to any questions.

Note 4: placing individuals at the centre of care planning and delivery contributes to valuing families' preferences and aiming to meet their expectations about birth regardless of the mode of delivery. A personalised approach to communication can reduce the risk of misunderstanding between healthcare professionals as well as service users as terms which are meaningful and supportive for one individual may not be helpful to another.

Note 5: Standard 4.4 states that practice supervisors *'are expected to appropriately raise and respond to student conduct and competence concerns and are supported in doing so'* (NMC, 2018b).

Summary: actions and learning for all

To facilitate effective learning and actions, it is important to view situations through different lenses (Brookfield, 1995), embracing every individual's perspective. This is crucial for all involved in creating conducive learning environments which feel safe, supportive and enable each person to flourish and develop. Key learning points may include:

EVIDENCE: Re:birth report, non-biased and inclusive educationally

EVIDENCE: the Code can be used by educators to assist students to 'understand what it means to be a registered professional and how keeping to the Code helps to achieve that' (NMC, 2018a), Standards framework for nursing and midwifery for education

VALUES: 6Cs compassion, communication

EVIDENCE: Part 2: SSSA (NMC, 2018b)

MODEL: reflective practice (Wain, 2017)

VALUE/EVIDENCE: freedom to speak up (NHS England, nd)

- the importance of enabling non-biased, non-judgemental and honest communication;

- enabling students to question and professionally challenge in an objective way to enhance their knowledge and learning;

- appreciating that what and how you communicate will affect the feelings of others and their internal well-being;

- practice placement areas need to demonstrate that they are delivering care based on evidence-based best practice;

- actively involving students in the processes of continuing professional development;

- the need for all individuals to understand the process of escalating any concerns and how to speak up regardless of their position.

Questions for reflection and discussion

1. How do you feel about supporting student learning in your own practice area? Why do you feel this way?

2. How do you think practice supervisor feedback can be used most effectively?

3. What in your view is the best way that learners can be supported when experiencing situations beyond their knowledge and skills?

4. What is your knowledge of the process and management when a concern is raised about student or supervisor actions in the practice learning environment?

5. Reflect on a recent interaction in your practice and consider your own actions as a student or supervisor and whether you took an objective and non-judgemental approach or were aware of any pre-existing bias.

6. Contemplate how you could improve your practice to ensure all parties are considered in an inclusive and supported way.

Helpful resources

Advance HE – www.advance-he.ac.uk

Centre for the Advancement of Interprofessional Education – www.caipe.org/resources/publications/caipe-publications/lindqvist-s-anderson-e-diack-l-reeves-s-2017-caipe-fellows-statement-integrative-care

PROMPT – www.promptmaternity.org/Pages/Category/training-model

References

Brookfield, S (1995) *Becoming a Critically Reflective Teacher*. San Francisco, CA: Jossey-Bass.

Gibbs, G (1988) *Learning by Doing: A Guide to Teaching and Learning Methods*. Oxford: Oxford Centre for Staff and Learning Development, Oxford Brookes University.

Hamilton, V, Baird, K and Fenwick, J (2020) Nurturing Autonomy in Student Midwives within a Student Led Antenatal Clinic. *Midwifery*, 33, 448–54.

Lindqvist, S, Anderson, E, Diack, L and Reeves, S (2017) CAIPE Fellows Statement on Integrative Care. [online] Available at: www.caipe.org/resources/publications/caipe-publications/lindqvist-s-anderson-e-diack-l-reeves-s-2017-caipe-fellows-statement-integrative-care (accessed 9 March 2023).

National Institute for Health and Care Excellence (NICE) (2017) *Intrapartum Care for Healthy Women and Babies*. CG 190. London. NICE.

NHS England (2016) *National Maternity Review. Better Births: Improving Outcomes of Maternity Services in England – A Five Year Forward View for Maternity Care*. [online] Available at: www.england.nhs.uk/wp-content/uploads/2016/02/national-maternity-review-report.pdf (accessed 19 December 2022).

Nursing & Midwifery Council (NMC) (2018a) *The Code: Professional Standards of Practice and Behaviour for Nurses, Midwives and Nursing Associates*. London: Nursing & Midwifery Council.

Nursing & Midwifery Council (NMC) (2018b) *Standards for Student Supervision and Assessment*. London: Nursing & Midwifery Council.

Nursing & Midwifery Council (NMC) (2018c) *Part 1: Standards Framework for Nursing and Midwifery for Education*. London: Nursing & Midwifery Council.

Nursing & Midwifery Council (NMC) (2019) Part 3: Standards for Pre-registration Midwifery Programmes. [online] Available at: www.nmc.org.uk/globalassets/sitedocuments/standards/standards-for-pre-registration-midwifery-programmes.pdf (accessed 14 APril 2023).

Ockenden, D (2022) *Findings, Conclusions and Essential Actions from the Independent Review of Maternity Services at The Shrewsbury and Telford Hospital NHS Trust*. London: HMSO.

Prompt Maternity Team (2017) *PROMPT Course Manual*. 3rd ed. Cambridge: Cambridge University Press.

Royal College of Anaesthetists (RCA) (2018) *Care of the Critically Ill Woman in Childbirth: Enhanced Maternal Care*. London: Royal College of Anaesthetists.

Royal College of Midwives (RCM) (2022) *Re:Birth Summary Report*. London: RCM. [online] Available at: www.rcm.org.uk/media/6180/rcm-rebirth-report.pdf (accessed 9 March 2023).

Royal College of Obstetricians and Gynaecologists (RCOG) (2016) *Prevention and Management of Postpartum Haemorrhage*. Green-top Guideline No. 52. [online] Available at: www.rcog.org.uk/guidance/browse-all-guidance/green-top-guidelines/prevention-and-management-of-postpartum-haemorrhage-green-top-guideline-no-52 (accessed 9 March 2023).

UNICEF, The Baby Friendly Initiative (nd) Baby Friendly Standards. [online] Available at: www.unicef.org.uk/babyfriendly/about/standards (accessed 9 March 2023).

Wain, A (2017) Learning Through Reflection. *British Journal of Midwifery*, 25(10): 662–6.

Case study 6
Katarzyna: when services are restricted

Jemma Thorne and Jo Knox

Introduction

In this case study we consider the relationships between different areas within the maternity setting, specifically exploring the hierarchy experienced between delivery suite and midwifery-led birthing unit (MLBU) colleagues. The case study includes a reflective account from a midwife who was rostered to work on the midwifery-led unit and is challenged when advocating to keep the midwife-led birthing unit open during a period of low staffing and high activity. It explores how this situation can increase hostility among the maternity team and the impact this has on their psychological safety. The case study closes with ideas for further actions to develop reflective skills, and suggestions for evidence-based enquiry and supportive exploration with colleagues.

The situation

As I walk the familiar steps towards the midwifery-led birthing unit (MLBU) for the start of my night shift, I wonder how long it will be before I get asked to work on the delivery suite. The answer is immediately: the decision has been made to close the MLBU due to reduced staffing across the maternity unit, and I am asked to attend the delivery suite for the duration of my shift. I pick up the cordless phone and close the door of the office, attaching the sign to say the MLBU is closed. As I leave, I am given a word of warning from the MLBU day staff, telling me who the co-ordinator on the delivery suite is tonight, thus preparing me for a challenging conversation, which would not have to take place if this were a free-standing birth unit.

> **EVIDENCE:** *free-standing birth units were described as more supportive and satisfying work environments, in which midwives could establish rewarding relationships with women and their families. In contrast, consultant-led units were frequently perceived negatively, particularly because of the dominance of a medical model of childbirth, a task-orientated approach to practice and an atmosphere of 'lots of criticism and no praise' (Hunter, 2004, p 255)*

When I arrive on the delivery suite and approach the shift co-ordinator, I ask not to be allocated to care for any women in active labour. I explain I would like to keep the MLBU open if any women call the unit and want to attend there for birth. I feel strongly about women being able to birth in

VALUES: autonomy and advocacy. 'Women planning birth in a midwifery unit and multiparous women planning birth at home experience fewer interventions than those planning birth in an obstetric unit with no impact on perinatal outcomes' (Birthplace in England Collaborative Group, 2012)

EVIDENCE: safe staffing: 'All trusts must maintain a clear escalation and mitigation policy where maternity staffing falls below the minimum staffing levels for all health professionals' (Ockenden report, 2022)

MODEL: hierarchy of decision making

THEORY: birth choices. The Nursing and Midwifery Council's Code (NMC, 2018) says that midwives must put the interests of women first and make their safety the main concern. This is their professional duty

their preferred environment, be this in their home, the MLBU or on the delivery suite. The co-ordinator makes it clear she wants me to stay on the delivery suite for the whole shift to support with the staffing issues, explaining that I would have no support on the MLBU if I chose to look after a woman in labour there by myself. I explain I feel confident to care for a woman in labour on the MLBU with the support of the senior midwifery care assistant (MCA) who is working the night shift and knowing I have my midwifery colleagues working on the nearby postnatal ward. If I were to pull the emergency buzzer, I know my colleagues would be there to support me. The co-ordinator's non-verbal communication clearly conveys she is not in agreement with my plan, and she allocates me to care for two postnatal women and their babies; these women have recently given birth and are currently required to stay on the delivery suite.

At 00:36 the MLBU telephone rings. I answer the phone to a woman named Katarzyna; she is a multiparous woman, her previous birth being a waterbirth on the MLBU. Katarzyna is contracting strongly every five minutes and is keen to attend the MLBU. I invite her in, explaining that an MCA will let me know when she arrives as I am currently working on the delivery suite.

The co-ordinator at this time is busy supporting another colleague with a vaginal breech and is not able to be disturbed. My two postnatal women remain on the delivery suite; one I can transfer to the postnatal ward, while the other needs to remain on the delivery suite. I ask my colleagues around me if anybody is happy to take over the care of the postnatal mother and her baby, who will remain on the delivery suite. I write the midwife's name on the whiteboard and hand over care. I transfer the other postnatal woman and baby to the postnatal ward, handing over care before returning to the MLBU.

At 01:12 Katarzyna arrives on the MLBU; she is clearly in established labour. The senior MCA on the MLBU has already prepared the birth environment: a birthing pool full of water, lights turned down low and LED flameless candles switched on. Within two hours of her arrival in the MLBU, Katarzyna gives birth to her baby boy in the water, the senior MCA answering my buzzer when the vertex becomes visible. I support Katarzyna in achieving her birth preferences, enabling her to birth in the environment she desired. She continues with a physiological birth of the placenta; she has an intact perineum and starts breastfeeding her son shortly after birth. As Katarzyna basks in her oxytocin, I leave the room with buzzer to hand to complete the documentation attached to the birth. The MCA heads to the kitchen to prepare the traditional post birth refreshments of tea and toast.

I telephone the delivery suite to inform the co-ordinator that the woman is now postnatal, and all is well. She tells me the unit remains busy and she is likely to require me back on the delivery suite before the end of the night shift. When I end the call, I convey the conversation to my MCA colleague. She has recently returned from the kitchen on the delivery suite and tells me the white board looks okay and there are midwives sitting around at the desk. In other words, there is no reason to request my return to the delivery suite.

I collect the equipment needed to complete the examination of the newborn: the trolley with weighing scales, tape measure, cot card and freshly drawn-up injection of vitamin K and cotton wool. I knock gently on the door, not wanting to disturb the tranquillity. Katarzyna looks up from her baby smiling, reporting that he has breastfed for half an hour and has now fallen asleep. I ask if I can weigh him and complete my checks; she nods and provides me with verbal consent to complete the newborn checks. We talk throughout the examination, with a small cry from the baby when I administer the vitamin K injection. From my examination I conclude that there are no abnormalities detected and he weighs 3.65 kg. Katarzyna and Davide nod in acknowledgement when I verbalise the weight.

VALUE: birth choices

When caring for Katarzyna postnatally, I regularly check in on her and her new baby, ensuring her physical and emotional needs are met. I give them time to be alone as a new family and absorb the oxytocin with their new son, not wanting to disturb those precious first hours of bonding, but equally wanting to ensure Katarzyna and baby are safe. I explain my plan of care at each point of contact, checking maternal observations, lochia and bladder care.

The documentation takes time, but can be completed outside the room, firstly finishing the paper notes followed by the electronic notes. It is 04:17 when I sit back in my chair to stretch and think about making myself a hot drink. The co-ordinator rings from the delivery suite asking me to return to care for a woman who is having her labour induced due to prolonged rupture of membranes (PROM). I explain that I still have a postnatal woman on the MLBU and need to have a break as well. She tells me the postnatal woman can be cared for by the senior MCA on the MLBU with support from the midwives on the nearby postnatal ward. I am tired and hang up the phone, relaying the conversation to my MCA colleague. She is disappointed that I will be returning to the delivery suite for the rest of the shift, but we also acknowledge this was expected. She is happy to care for Katarzyna, knowing she can support with feeding while waiting for the newborn infant physical examination (NIPE) before the discharge home. I knock on Katarzyna's door to let her know I will be working on the delivery suite for the rest of the shift but that she will be in the very capable hands of the MCA. Katarzyna and Davide are grateful for their care from me and thank me for being part of the birth.

I make myself a drink and take it across to the delivery suite with me, making a clear visual point that I still need to have a refreshment break. The co-ordinator tells me what room I will be in and that the midwife from the antenatal ward is waiting for me so that she can hand over the woman's care. For the rest of my shift, I focus my mindset on caring for the woman undergoing induction of labour, trying not to feel frustrated by the co-ordinator.

EVIDENCE: Smith et al (2009) explored healthcare professionals' views about safety in maternity care with respondents noting a consequence of being constantly overstretched at work with no time for breaks: many midwives admitted to being tired and burnt out, and therefore more likely to make errors

At the end of my shift, I walk slowly back to the MLBU to hand over care of Katarzyna to the day staff. The MCA has provided excellent care and the day staff are already arranging who will undertake the NIPE and discharge them both home. The day staff let me vent about my night shift and being called to the delivery suite to help their workload and the maternity services.

Reflections

What saddened me most about this discussion was that I was expecting it. I knew as I walked across to the delivery suite that I would be challenged on my preference to keep the midwifery-led unit open. I know on a different shift with a different co-ordinator I would not have needed to have this conversation. When attempting to escalate my concerns regarding closing the unit, my apprehension was disregarded, and priority was placed on the women on the delivery suite and not those who would like to attend the MLBU.

I felt this co-ordinator's behaviour impacted on the psychological safety of the maternity unit as a whole. The co-ordinator's disregard for not allowing me to express my opinions and feelings made me feel that because they were deemed more senior than me due to their co-ordinator role, my concerns were without value. They made it explicit that their decision was final, thus not empowering me to speak up. I felt frustrated by this conversation with the co-ordinator and disappointed in their attitude.

When reflecting on this conversation, it triggered me to question if this shift co-ordinator lacked the confidence to care for a low-risk woman in labour themself. Did they genuinely did not view it feasible for me to feel confident in this area rather than it being an issue of safety and women's choice? I recognise that keeping birthplace options available to all is an area I feel strongly and passionately about, and know I feel equally disappointed when a woman wanting a homebirth is asked to attend the unit.

I made sure the women I was caring for remained in safe care, handing them over to different midwives to ensure that their care continued. Shared professional decision making (SPDM) is becoming more widely used within nursing in the UK, but it seems less well used in midwifery. In this situation the band 6 midwives made the decision

MODEL: restorative clinical supervision. Carter (2022) discusses the protection of restorative clinical supervision being fundamental in supporting a competent, resilient and psychologically safe workforce

EVIDENCE: Kline (2020) advises that 'inclusion' should be a core competency for healthcare leadership values, and that inclusivity and compassion create 'psychologically safe workplaces' by building healthier relationships between staff and reducing patient mortality

VALUE: the Ockenden report (2022) states that all trusts must develop and maintain a conflict of clinical opinion policy to support staff members in being able to escalate their clinical concerns regarding a woman's care in case of disagreement between healthcare professionals

EVIDENCE: Keating and Fleming (2009) conducted a small-scale study with the objective of exploring midwives' experiences of facilitating normal birth in an obstetric-led unit and concluded that midwifery knowledge and practice are subsumed within a birth culture where medical expertise and technology are valued

MODEL: SPDM is intended to empower staff at all levels to initiate and drive improvement (Trueland, 2022)

VALUE: Standards of Proficiency (NMC, 2019)

MODEL: workforce planning. Birthrate Plus is a workforce planning and decision-making system for assessing the needs of women for midwifery care throughout pregnancy, labour and the postnatal period both in hospital and community settings. The methodology has been in constant use in the UK since 1988, but one could question whether this methodology is now outdated with maternity care transforming significantly since its development. Ball and Washbrook (2010, p 730), who were heavily involved in the creation of Birthrate Plus, explored the changes in responsibilities of midwives: 'The most recent studies indicate that community midwives are increasingly involved with public health initiatives and hospital midwives are doing more of the work previously undertaken by junior doctors'

VALUE: Changing Childbirth (DH, 1993) presented midwives with the ongoing challenge of developing a woman-centred service within an environment underpinned by hierarchical control. Martin and Bull (2005) explored the influence of the senior midwife in decision making in maternity care and concluded that a senior midwife was able to influence decisions, many of which should be woman centred. When a hierarchy exists, a senior midwife is likely to lead care, even when another midwife has built up a picture of a woman's birth values and preferences

between themselves to reallocate care and workload without the co-ordinator being involved.

I always felt that I was adhering to the six domains of the NMC standards by ensuring safe and effective midwifery care and being an accountable and autonomous professional midwife.

However, I am not a co-ordinator and reflect on whether I perceive my knowledge and experience to be at a similar level to theirs, when in fact it is not. I am focused on advocating for one woman to achieve the physiological birth she desires, whereas the delivery suite co-ordinator is considering the whole of the maternity unit. I am pleased I was able to advocate for Katarzyna and provide personalised and women-centred care but wonder if it was to the detriment of other women. The co-ordinator is continuously reviewing the needs of all and making plans for the ongoing inductions of labour on the antenatal ward.

In 1993, the Department of Health (DH) produced *Changing Childbirth*, requesting the provision for more choice, continuity and control for women during pregnancy and childbirth. This paper has been much discussed over the years in educational programmes and clinical settings. *Changing Childbirth* was produced 30 years ago, but the same ongoing challenges of supporting women to achieve their decisions in a hierarchical system remains. In 2017, *Better Births*, a national maternity review, was produced, with a vision *'for maternity services across England… to become safer, more personalised, kinder, professional and more family friendly; where every woman has access to information to enable her to make decisions about her care; and where she and her baby can access support that is centred around their individual needs and circumstances'*. It remains to be seen if the transformation activity from the *Better Births* report will deliver on its promise.

I also now reflect on the Ockenden report (Ockenden, 2022) and feel torn as to whether being an experienced midwife working through the Normal Birth campaign presented by the Royal College of Midwives (RCM) has set a precedent in my mind for my boundaries within midwifery care. The RCM Normal Birth campaign was withdrawn in 2017, but I question whether it had already caused damage.

Actions

I took time to reflect on the situation and developed an action plan which I could implement if the situation arose again.

The staff on the preceding shift had 'warned' me about who the co-ordinator for the night was. This meant that I had preconceived notions about the potential confrontation I would encounter. I was already feeling defensive about trying to keep patient choice as the priority when I knew that this would be challenged due to the staffing deficit across the unit.

On reflection, if this situation were to occur again, I would like to have an open conversation with the co-ordinator. I would explain that I understand that staff safety is always a priority and paramount and that there may be other ways to maintain safe levels for all. For example, if I were to be positioned in the maternity assessment unit where I could triage phone calls and women, I would be available to support the MLBU if the need arises. I also need to acknowledge the responsibility of the delivery suite co-ordinator and be respectful.

Questions for reflection and discussion

1. If the MLBU is closed due to safety on the delivery suite, where there are not enough midwives to provide safe one-to-one labour care, would patient safety or choice take priority and why?

2. How do you feel about challenging somebody deemed more senior than you within your professional boundaries? What tools could you use to aid you to professionally challenge someone?

3. Would you have made the choice to escalate your concerns to the manager on call rather than challenging the co-ordinator yourself? If yes, why?

4. If you were the co-ordinator and had to make decisions about workload, skill mix and the women across the maternity unit, would you have made similar choices and how would you have communicated them?

5. How would you feel if Katarzyna had not been advocated for in her birth choices and been given only the option of delivery suite?

6. Was it appropriate for Katarzyna to be cared for by an MCA, and where does accountability lie?

Helpful resources

Choice of birth and birth places – www.birthrights.org.uk/factsheets/choice-of-place-of-birth/ #choosewhere

International Confederation of Midwives – www.internationalmidwives.org/icm-news/history-of-midwifery-the-role-of-advocacy-in-midwifery.html

References

Ball, J and Washbrook, M (2010) Birthrate Plus: Using Ratios for Maternity Workforce Planning. *British Journal of Midwifery*, 18(11): 724–30.

Birthplace in England Collaborative Group (2012) Perinatal and Maternal Outcomes by Planned Place of Birth for Healthy Women with Low-Risk Pregnancies: The Birthplace in England National Prospective Cohort Study. *British Medical Journal*, 344(840): 17.

Carter, V (2022) Can Restorative Clinical Supervision Positively Impact the Psychological Safety of Midwives and Nurses? *British Journal of Nursing*, 31(15): 818–20.

Department of Health (1993) Report of the Expert Maternity Group: Changing Childbirth (Cumberlege Report). London: HMSO.

Hunter, B (2004) Emotion Work and Boundary Maintenance in Hospital-based Midwifery. *Midwifery*, 21: 253–66.

Keating, A and Fleming, V (2009) Midwives' Experience of Facilitating Normal Birth in an Obstetric-led Unit: A Feminist Perspective. *Midwifery*, 25(5): 515–27.

Kline, R (2020) *Those Who Cannot Do So Cannot Be Entrusted to Lead the NHS*. [online] Available at: https://blogs.bmj.com/bmjleader/2020/07/26/those-who-cannot-do-so-cannot-be-entrusted-to-lead-the-nhs-by-roger-kline (accessed 9 March 2023).

Martin, C and Bull, P (2005) Measuring Social Influence of a Senior Midwife on Decision-Making in Maternity Care: An Experimental Study. *Journal of Community and Applied Social Psychology*, 15: 120–6.

NHS England (2016) *National Maternity Review. Better Births: Improving Outcomes of Maternity Services in England – A Five Year Forward View for Maternity Care*. [online] Available at: www.engl and.nhs.uk/wp-content/uploads/2016/02/national-maternity-review-report.pdf (accessed 19 December 2022).

Nursing & Midwifery Council (NMC) (2018) *The Code: Professional Standards of Practice and Behaviour for Nurses, Midwives and Nursing Associates*. London: Nursing & Midwifery Council.

Nursing & Midwifery Council (NMC) (2019) *Standards of Proficiency for Midwives*. [online] Available at: www.nmc.org.uk/globalassets/sitedocuments/standards/standards-of-proficiency-for-midwives. pdf (accessed 23 January 2023)

Ockenden, D (2022) *Findings, Conclusions and Essential Actions from the Independent Review of Maternity Services at The Shrewsbury and Telford Hospital NHS Trust*. London: HMSO.

Smith, A, Dixon, A and Page, L (2009) Health-Care Professionals' Views about Safety in Maternity Services: A Qualitative Study. *Midwifery*, 25(1): 21–31.

Trueland, J (2022) Ditching Hierarchy in Nursing: Does Shared Decision-making Work? *Nursing Management*, UK, 29(3): 13–15.

Case study 7
Amira: refer or defer?

Jayne Needham and Jo Knox

Introduction

This case study explores the role of the midwife in supporting women with cardiac complexities in pregnancy. These complexities in pregnancy are rare but remain a leading cause of maternal death, largely due to acquired heart disease associated with co-morbidities such as obesity and hypertension (Knight et al, 2022). The dilemmas and decisions encountered in this scenario include recognition of the signs and symptoms of ill health without applying a pregnancy bias, exploring the nature of the problem, investigating clinical factors and ensuring appropriate timely referral. The dilemma of supporting pregnancy and providing guidance to women whose lives are impacted by poor economic circumstances and the associated issues this brings is also highlighted in this case study. It is worth noting almost half the women who died from cardiovascular causes between 2018 and 2020 were resident in the most deprived quintile of geographical areas in the UK (Knight et al, 2022). The clinical scenario presented below unfolds over two consultations.

The initial consultation

I met 34 year-old Amira when she was 12 weeks' pregnant in her fifth pregnancy. Amira is of British Pakistani heritage. I completed the initial booking consultation according to National Institute for Health and Care Excellence (NICE, 2017) guidance. This consultation comprises a full medical, obstetric, family and social history. During the appointment Amira told me that she is a single parent working part time as a cleaner in her local public house. She struggles financially to care for her four other children aged between two and seven. Amira consented to a check on her carbon monoxide levels, using a handheld carbon monoxide monitor, which indicated that her levels were raised. This initiated a conversation about smoking in which she admitted to smoking 20 cigarettes per day. I explained the benefits of giving up smoking in pregnancy, but she felt it was her only pleasure in life. She declined the offer of a referral to the smoking cessation service after I had talked about the support that could be offered to help her stop smoking. Amira understands her diet is not ideal, as sometimes she cannot afford to eat and prioritises her children when planning meals, sometimes going without food herself. I talked to her about assistance available for fresh food vouchers and how she can get these from the government Healthy Start website. We also talked about food banks available locally and how referrals can be made to these.

MODEL: personalised care

Amira has a body mass index (BMI) of 35 and I noted that following her last pregnancy she had a diagnosis of type 2 diabetes and takes oral metformin daily. Her HbA1c levels have not been checked since she found out that she was pregnant. Her diet of mainly high-fat/high-carbohydrate foods may impact the HbA1c levels in her blood and consequently affect her diabetes. Amira told me that her father died from a heart attack when he was 37. Due to the risk factors for cardiac disease that I identified, I explained to Amira that I would like to refer her to the obstetric team for her care to be consultant-led, meaning that she would be seen by the team in the hospital. This will be beneficial to her as she will receive specialist advice regarding her diabetes and a possible referral to a cardiologist for an expert opinion regarding lifestyle choices, family history and the possibility of acquired cardiac disease.

After the booking consultation

MODEL: Stepping up to Public Health. The Royal College of Midwives' health promotion model is designed to enable midwives to address public health aspects of care at each contact with a client during pregnancy, birth and postnatal care

Reflections

MODEL: risk assessment

VALUE: professional scope of practice – 'respect the skills, expertise and contributions of your colleagues, referring matters to them where appropriate' (the Code, NMC, 2018)

I felt conscious that the allotted time for the booking appointment was too short to explore in any real depth with Amira the many issues the consultation had raised. I considered her diabetes and lifestyle factors, including her family history, and decided to organise a referral to an obstetrician. I also felt that Amira may not be fully aware of the risks of smoking when pregnant and the influence her diet and family history may have on her continuing health.

EVIDENCE: risk factors for cardiac disease (Boyle and Bothamley, 2018)

Actions

I completed the referral for Amira to see an obstetrician and made certain that she understood why I was making the referral. The threshold for referral with the lifestyle, medical and family history should be low (Knight et al, 2022). I also asked her if she would be able to get to the hospital for the appointment.

MODEL: risk assessment

VALUES: empathy and compassion (Krause et al, 2020), person-centred care (Santana et al, 2018)

The 35-week midwife consultation

Amira was seen in a joint clinic by an endocrinologist and an obstetrician when she was 18 weeks' pregnant and had a cardiology appointment at 20 weeks' gestation. Amira felt she would like to continue to see her community midwife at regular intervals for continuity of care and to save her costs on public transport to the hospital.

VALUES: empathy and compassion (Krause et al, 2020), person-centred care (Santana et al, 2018)

MODEL: multi-professional working

Today Amira is attending the 35-week appointment and is visibly short of breath (SOB). I question Amira to ascertain whether this was a new symptom and whether she feels SOB at rest. I note that her last haemoglobin was within normal limits. Amira tells me that she saw her GP last week as she had a dry cough and the GP prescribed antibiotics for a possible chest infection. However, the antibiotics have not improved the breathlessness or the cough.

Amira says that she has been SOB for about a week and recently at night feels the need to open the window and get air from the outside. She is rubbing her chest and comments that her chest is painful. I ask her to describe the chest pain and whether it is stabbing, aching, heavy, intermittent or constant pain. She explains it is like a weight on her chest, which is worse at night when she is in bed. I ask Amira if she is still smoking, and she replies that she often has a cigarette instead of eating and she feels that it helps to reduce the breathlessness and her hunger. At this point it is important that I consider all potential diagnoses.

EVIDENCE: questions to assess chest pain (Boyle and Bothamley, 2018)

MODEL: differential diagnosis.
Richardson et al (2000, p 64)
describe differential diagnosis
as 'considering the clinical
findings before making a final
diagnosis'

EVIDENCE: normal cardiac
physiology in pregnancy
(European Society of Cardiology
(ESC) Guidelines, 2018)

EVIDENCE: risk factors for
cardiac disease (British Heart
Foundation, 2022)

I assimilate the symptoms to establish a working diagnosis while considering normal physiological changes that occur in pregnancy; this method is called differential diagnosis. Pregnancy produces changes in the cardiovascular system to meet the increased metabolic demands of the mother and fetus. Blood volume and cardiac output increases by 30–50 per cent, which reaches a peak at around 24–28 weeks' gestation and remain high until the term of the pregnancy. Furthermore, there is an increase in heart rate of 10–20 beats per minute (bpm). Prostaglandins and progesterone decrease the peripheral vascular resistance and blood pressure. The prevalence of coronary heart disease in women is increasingly related to changing patterns of lifestyle, including cigarette smoking, diabetes, sedentary lifestyle, obesity and stress. Risk factors that cannot be modified include family history, age and ethnic background.

Amira's risk factors for developing coronary heart disease are diabetes, smoking, increased BMI, family history and ethnic background. In the most recent MBRRACE-UK report (Knight et al, 2022), heart disease remains a leading cause of maternal death in pregnancy or immediately following pregnancy. It is therefore vital that maternity healthcare professionals are aware of the common risk factors and take appropriate actions.

EVIDENCE: Royal College
of Physicians (2019) Toolkit
15: managing acute medical
problems in pregnancy

Chest pain red flags to be aware of are pain requiring opioids, pain radiating to the arm, shoulder, back or jaw, sudden onset, tearing or exertional chest pain. Other clinical clues may include chest pain associated with haemoptysis, breathlessness, syncope or abnormal neurology.

Reflections

I am aware that at 35 weeks' gestation Amira may have symptoms of anaemia, which include shortness of breath, so this needs to be excluded. I check her blood results from samples taken at 28 weeks and they were all within normal limits. This increases my concern about Amira because of the chest pain coupled with SOB. I am aware that SOB is one of the most common presenting symptoms for those with heart disease. However, it is also a common presenting symptom for respiratory disease and sepsis, as well as being a normal pregnancy symptom. I am aware that unexplained SOB should always be investigated, especially if associated with paroxysmal nocturnal dyspnoea as in Amira's case. Chest pain is also a common presenting symptom in those with cardiac disease; however, chest pain may also be associated with musculoskeletal pain, reflux, pneumothorax and pulmonary embolism. As a midwife, I am aware that I need to act within my scope of practice and be aware of my limitations and refer to the multi-disciplinary team if complexities are recognised.

EVIDENCE: NG121: Intrapartum care for women with existing medical conditions or obstetric complications and their babies (NICE, 2019)

THEORY: the Code (NMC, 2018)

I reflected on the findings. My dilemma was do I refer or defer? I must consider if it is it possible that a 34 year-old pregnant woman could be exhibiting the signs and symptoms of a myocardial infarction. However, I am aware that the recent enquiry into maternal death in the United Kingdom stated that between 2018 and 2020, 61 women died of heart disease (Knight et al, 2022). Many of the deaths were in women aged between 30 and 34; 29 of the women who died were living in the most deprived areas of the UK and 54 had no known pre-existing cardiac problems. Knight et al (2022) suggest that ischaemic heart disease is often overlooked in the maternity population but there does need to be a high index of suspicion if risk factors are present. I am an autonomous practitioner and the knowledge, experience and skills I have direct me to the conclusion that I need to refer Amira to the hospital.

Amira has a high respiration rate, low oxygen saturations, tachycardia and looks unwell. My professional opinion is this unlikely to be a chest infection as Amira is apyrexial and does not have a productive cough. Also, it is probably not a pulmonary embolism as Amira does not have haemoptysis. Coupled with the clinical findings and lifestyle choices, I am led to believe that Amira may have ischaemic heart disease and may be displaying symptoms of a myocardial infarction. My decision was therefore to transfer her to hospital as soon as possible via a paramedic ambulance. I am acutely aware that as a midwife I have the responsibility of referring on anything that is outside the role of the midwife. The consequences of deferring in Amira's case could be catastrophic.

Actions

I am very concerned about Amira and how quickly she may deteriorate. Pregnant women can compensate, meaning that they appear slightly unwell, and their vital signs begin to be outside of the normal limits, but then they become suddenly seriously unwell. It is therefore paramount that I effectively and competently undertake an assessment of the cardiovascular system without delay. Having previously worked as a nurse I believe that all community midwives should be trained to manage these situations and if they do not feel competent to do so they must escalate and seek support from a colleague who can. I use the gold-standard ABCDE approach to assess Amira. I considered each of the aspects.

VALUE: autonomous practice

EVIDENCE: the deteriorating patient (Resuscitation Council UK, 2021)

- **Airway** – Amira's airway is clear, with her sitting in an upright position receiving oxygen at 10 l/min from an oxygen cylinder via a rebreathe mask. An upright sitting position seems sensible as Amira is having some difficulty breathing.

- **Breathing** – her respiratory rate is 28 per minute, oxygen saturations 89 per cent on air. Respiratory rate is considered to be one of the most sensitive indicators of the development of critical illness (Grady et al, 2007). A respiratory rate above 24 breaths per minute is a red flag and is a serious cause for concern.

- **Circulation** – blood pressure 108/68, pulse 118 bpm, temperature 37.6°C, prolonged capillary refill time >2 seconds. A prolonged capillary refill time may indicate poor peripheral perfusion (Woodrow, 2018).

- **Disability** – alert, sweating and anxious. The use of AVPU assessment tool (alert, responds to voice, responds to pain or unconscious) assesses the consciousness level.

- **Exposure** – Amira is evidently using accessory muscles for respiration; fetal heart auscultated 165 bpm, fetal movements felt by Amira.

I document all the observations on a MEOWS (Modified Early Obstetric Warning Score) chart, resulting in a score of 5. Any score between 1 and 3 requires medical review.

THEORY: RCOG Green-top Guideline No. 56: Maternal collapse in pregnancy and the puerperium (Chu et al, 2020)

Regular monitoring of vital signs and documentation on a MEOWS chart helps with early recognition of alterations and deterioration in a woman's condition. The use of the MEOWS score prompts early referral to an appropriate practitioner and escalation of clinical interventions. This can lead to early intervention and in turn reduce morbidity and mortality. I use the electrocardiogram (ECG) machine in the GP surgery and ask the staff in the surgery to call a paramedic ambulance immediately and let me know when they have completed the task and if there are any updates on arrival times of the ambulance. It is vitally important that the surgery staff 'close the loop' by coming back to me and informing me that they have completed the tasks so that I am aware of what is happening in terms of transferring Amira to hospital but also so that I can keep the staff up to date on Amira's condition. The findings of the ECG will aid diagnosis of myocardial infarction or pulmonary embolism.

MODEL: emergency management – feedback loop

I provide a full explanation of my findings to Amira and ask her if she would like me to call anyone on her behalf. Her children are being looked after by her next-door neighbour. I complete an analysis of Amira's pain symptoms using a pain score. I ask Amira questions to establish the site and intensity of the pain. Such questions include: When did the pain begin? Has it happened before? Is the pain there all the time? Does anything relieve the pain? How would she describe the pain? I undertake a 12-lead ECG (electrocardiograph); as I am in a GP surgery, there is an ECG machine available; this may not be the case in a health centre.

THEORY: pain assessment tools

Using an oxygen saturation monitor, I undertake continuous oxygen saturation monitoring and administer oxygen titrated to Amira's oxygen saturations.

MODEL: assessment of the cardiac system (Boyle and Bothamley, 2018)

I record observations of Amira's vital signs every 15 minutes, including calculation of the MEOWS score; it is important to note that a thready pulse can be indicative of poor cardiac output.

I contact the midwifery co-ordinator on the labour ward to inform them of Amira's condition and probable transfer to the cardiology department at the hospital. In this situation the paramedics will divert directly to the cardiology department.

MODEL: multi-professional working

Questions for reflection and discussion

1. Consider what you know about cardiac disease and pregnancy and whether you feel you would require additional training to manage this situation.

2. What does the most recent MBRRACE-UK report suggest about cardiac disease and its prevalence?

3. Consider how to communicate the urgency of the situation to the multi-disciplinary team. What are the key red flags identified?

4. How would you allay Amira's anxiety while also highlighting the seriousness of the situation?

5. What sort of debriefing may be suitable for Amira following this episode?

6. What may be the consequences regarding her lifestyle and support she may require following a diagnosis of a cardiac event?

Helpful resources

Chu, J, Johnston, T A and Geoghegan, J (2020) Maternal Collapse in Pregnancy and the Puerperium. *BJOG 2020*, 127: e14–e52.

Healthy Start: guidance on the government Healthy Start scheme – www.gov.uk/healthy-start

MBRRACE: a continuing professional development course for midwives based on the MBRRACE reports – www.npeu.ox.ac.uk/mbrrace-uk/mbrrace-online-course/maternal-course

Royal College of Midwives (RCM) (2017) *Stepping up to Public Health: A New Maternity Model for Women and Families, Midwives and Maternity Support Workers* – www.rcm.org.uk/media/3165/stepping-up-to-public-health.pdf

References

Boyle, M and Bothamley, J (2018) *Critical Care Assessment by Midwives.* Oxford: Routledge.

British Heart Foundation (2022) Coronary Heart Disease. [online] Available at: www.bhf.org.uk/informationsupport/conditions/coronary-heart-disease (accessed 9 March 2023).

Chu, J, Johnston, T A and Geoghegan, J on behalf of the Royal College of Obstetricians and Gynaecologists (2020) Maternal Collapse in Pregnancy and the Puerperium. *British Journal of Obstetrics and Gynaecology.* [online] Available at: https://obgyn.onlinelibrary.wiley.com/doi/pdf/10.1111/1471-0528.15995 (accessed 14 April 2023).

European Society of Cardiology (2018) Guidelines for the Management of Cardiovascular Diseases During Pregnancy. *European Heart Journal*, 39: 3165–241.

Grady, K, Howell, C and Cox, C (eds) (2007) *Managing Obstetric Emergencies and Trauma: The MOET Course.* 2nd ed. London: RCOG.

Knight, M, Bunch, K, Patel, R, Shakespeare, J, Kotnis, R, Kenyon, S and Kurinczuk, J J (eds) (2022) *Saving Lives, Improving Mothers' Care Core Report: Lessons Learned to Inform Maternity Care from the UK and Ireland Confidential Enquiries into Maternal Deaths and Morbidity 2018–20.* Oxford: National Perinatal Epidemiology Unit, University of Oxford.

Krause, S, Minnie, C and Coetzee, S (2020) The Characteristics of Compassionate Care During Childbirth According to Midwives: A Qualitative Descriptive Inquiry. *BMC Pregnancy and Childbirth*, 20: 304.

National Institute for Health and Care Excellence (NICE) (2017) *Intrapartum Care for Healthy Women and Babies*. CG 190. London. NICE.

National Institute for Health and Care Excellence (NICE) (2019) Intrapartum Care for Women with Existing Medical Conditions or Obstetric Complications and Their Babies. NG121. [online] Available at: www.nice.org.uk/guidance/ng121 (accessed 9 March 2023).

Nursing & Midwifery Council (NMC) (2018) *The Code: Professional Standards of Practice and Behaviour for Nurses, Midwives and Nursing Associates.* London: Nursing & Midwifery Council.

Resuscitation Council UK (2021) The ABCDE Approach: The Deteriorating Patient. [online] Available at: www.resus.org.uk/library/abcde-approach# (accessed 9 March 2023).

Richardson, W S, Glasziou, P and Polashenski, W (2000) A New Arrival: Evidence about Differential Diagnosis. *BMJ Evidence-Based Medicine*, 5: 164–5.

Royal College of Physicians (2019) *Acute Care Toolkit 15: Managing Acute Medical Problems in Pregnancy.* London: Royal College of Physicians.

Santana, M, Manalili, K, Jolley, R, Zekinsky, S, Quan, H and Mingshan, L (2018) How to Practice Person Centred Care: A Conceptual Framework. *Health Expectations*, 21: 429–40.

Woodrow, P (2018) *Intensive Care Nursing: A Framework for Practice.* London: Routledge.

Part 3

Personalising care

Case study 8
Sara: 'return it to how it was...'

Georgina Sosa and Juliet Albert

This case study explores the roles and responsibilities of a midwife working with a woman who has previously undergone female genital mutilation (FGM). The dilemma is presented by the wishes of the husband, who wants the infibulation reinstated after the birth in direct contravention of the law. The midwife's decisions and communication are carefully articulated to ensure that she takes account of her legal responsibility. FGM is illegal in the UK and there is a mandatory reporting responsibility for all health professionals who encounter a woman or girl who has undergone FGM or is at risk of this.

The situation

Sara gave birth to a baby girl on a Friday at 15:16. The birth was intimate as Sara had her husband Karim with her and an interpreter, June. June shared that she had first met Sara at ten weeks' gestation, and she always tried to be present for her antenatal appointments. I welcomed June's presence and I was also relieved she knew Sara and had worked with the FGM specialist midwives.

The documentation showed that Sara started discussions about FGM at her booking assessment. She was then referred to a FGM specialist midwife who had expert knowledge and experience of caring for FGM survivors, who would ask the appropriate questions to improve health, labour and birth outcomes. The FGM specialist midwife performed a genital examination and classified Sara's genital cutting as type 3b. The FGM specialist midwife recorded that she had completed the enhanced dataset and discussed safeguarding. The FGM specialist midwife had not reported the FGM to the police because although Sara had FGM, she was over 18 years old. In England and Wales, regulated healthcare professionals have a statutory

VALUE: professional accountability. Female Genital Mutilation Act 2003 (England, Wales, and Northern Ireland); the Prohibition of Female Genital Mutilation (Scotland) Act 2005 (HM Government, 2020)

MODEL: continuity of care: language barriers have been highlighted as significantly compromising care when supporting women with FGM (Evans et al, 2019a, 2019b)

VALUE: confidentiality, stigma. Childbearing women can be cautious of interpreters, particularly around confidentiality. Additionally, interpreters will hold their own views concerning FGM and this can bias the health options discussed (WHO, 2018)

MODEL: person-centred care. All women should be asked at the booking interview whether they have experienced genital cutting while also asking about their medical and surgical history (RCOG, 2015)

MODEL: typology of FGM. See Table 8.1 adapted from Care of Women and Girls Living with Female Genital Mutilation: A Clinical Handbook (WHO, 2018). The documentation also included a diagram and a discussion about the benefits of antenatal deinfibulation, which is a midline incision (usually anteriorly) to cut open the bridge of scar tissue covering the urethra and vaginal opening until the urethra is visualised (WHO, 2018) duty to report 'known' cases of FGM in girls aged under 18 directly to the police (mandatory reporting duty). 'Known' cases are when a girl herself discloses that she has undergone FGM or where a professional observes evidence on a girl's genitals that she may have been cut. In Scotland and Northern Ireland, a child safeguarding referral should be made (HM Government, 2020).

> **MODEL: safeguarding.** There is a requirement to share information with NHS Digital whenever a woman or girl with FGM presents to an NHS acute or mental health Trust or GP surgery in England (NHS Digital, 2020)

FGM type	Description
Type 1	Partial or total removal of the clitoral glans and/or the prepuce. Sometimes known as clitoridectomy.
	Type Ia: Removal of the clitoral hood or prepuce only.
	Type Ib: Removal of the clitoral glans with the prepuce.
Type 2	Partial or total removal of the clitoral glans and the labia minora, with or without excision of the labia majora. Sometimes known as excision.
	Type IIa: Removal of the labia minora only.
	Type IIb: Partial or total removal of the clitoral glans and labia minora.
	Type IIc: Partial or total removal of the clitoral glans, labia minora and labia majora.
Type 3	Narrowing of the vaginal orifice with creation of a covering seal by cutting and appositioning the labia minora and/or the labia majora, with or without excision of the clitoral glans. Sometimes known as infibulation or pharaonic circumcision.
	Type IIIa: Removal and apposition of the labia minora.
	Type IIIb: Removal and apposition of the labia majora.
Type 4	All other harmful procedures to the female genitalia for non-medical purposes, including Gishiri cuts, pricking, piercing, incising, scraping and cauterisation and labial elongation.

Table 8.1 Adapted World Health Organization classification of FGM types

Realising that a deinfibulation (the process of cutting open the infibulation) in labour would be required, I started to question who would perform the procedure and when. I spoke to the delivery suite co-ordinator Deborah for support, and she asked whether the instructions specified that an obstetrician should perform the deinfibulation.

The maternity records specified that a trained midwife or obstetrician could perform the deinfibulation because there were no cysts, keloid scarring or other complex presentations. Additionally, the deinfibulation could be completed under local or epidural anaesthesia depending on Sara's preference. Deborah advised that she would perform the deinfibulation near the end of the first stage of labour with Sara's consent.

VALUE: professional accountability

I wondered why Sara had not had a deinfibulation in pregnancy. This would have been preferable as it would have been planned with a skilled person she knew. Sara shared that she was nervous about deferring her deinfibulation until labour. Sara said that she had contemplated having the deinfibulation procedure in the pregnancy, but she just could not bring herself to do it. Even the frequent urine infections could not sway her. Sara said she was terrified it would bring her back to that four year-old girl being held down and cut with no anaesthetic and wanted to defer it for as long as possible. I reassured Sara that she was in safe hands. I had received FGM training, and the delivery suite co-ordinator Deborah had experience in performing deinfibulations.

EVIDENCE: when deinfibulation is delayed until labour there is a higher risk of episiotomy, instrumental birth, caesarean section and longer hospital stay (Albert et al, 2015)

MODEL: psychological care

EVIDENCE: the majority of FGM is carried out on children between 5 and 12 years old and often by a traditional circumciser who has no formal medical training and may be using non-sterile equipment (Jones and Albert, 2021)

When assessing and supporting Sara in labour, I was mindful about the risk of flashbacks that Sara mentioned. I thought carefully about my words and body language. I wanted Sara to know that I was there to offer her holistic support encompassing both her physical and mental well-being. I wanted to gain her trust and was aware that performing vaginal examinations would be uncomfortable and potentially traumatic for Sara. When discussing the reasons for vaginal examinations, it was agreed that we would keep them to a minimum. I wondered if there was anything else I should be considering to be culturally safe (Evans et al, 2019b).

VALUE: avoid being judgemental. Instead show empathy (WHO, 2018) and gain consent for procedures (NMC, 2018)

VALUE: shared decision making

A deinfibulation was performed by Deborah with consent towards the end of the first stage of labour. She discussed the procedure and the physiological changes due to the deinfibulation although they had previously been discussed in the antenatal consultations with the FGM specialist midwife. These physiological changes following the deinfibulation included the genital area looking different; when passing urine it will flow faster and sound louder; there may also appear to be more menstrual blood than before and women may notice more vaginal discharge (WHO, 2018). The discussion and deinfibulation procedure occurred in between contractions and labour observations. Sara asked for her husband to leave the room. The interpreter was happy to remain in the room and support Sara throughout the deinfibulation, holding her hand and translating. During the deinfibulation procedure, Deborah stopped cutting the bridge of scar tissue when she visualised the urinary meatus. Deborah explained she would wait for a contraction to pass so she had more time to take great care so that she did not inadvertently cut into the urinary meatus. Deborah had a catheter ready if needed. Once the deinfibulation procedure was complete, Deborah checked the raw edges. There was a small amount of blood oozing initially that was seen on the gauze swab, which stopped within a couple of minutes. Sara had been counselled during pregnancy that over-sewing the edges would reduce bleeding, risk of infection and prevent the edges re-fusing post-partum. Deborah explained that the suturing would occur following birth as stitches could restrict the tissue stretching for the birth. Deborah then turned to me and explained that now the deinfibulation had been performed, the RCOG (2015) guidelines should be followed that stipulate the assessment for episiotomy should be completed. A routine episiotomy should not be performed for women with any of the four types of FGM. It is possible that an episiotomy may be required due to scarring and reduced elasticity of the introitus.

> EVIDENCE: once deinfibulation is performed, assessment for episiotomy should be completed. A routine episiotomy should not be performed for women with any of the four types of FGM. It is possible that an episiotomy may be required due to scarring and reduced elasticity of the introitus (RCOG, 2015)

When birth was imminent, I asked Deborah to attend as the second midwife so that I could receive affirmation about my episiotomy assessment. I kept watching the perineum and looking up at Deborah to double check, but the perineum kept stretching and then before I knew it, the baby's head was out. I noted a first-degree tear following the birth of a baby girl.

Once the placenta had been delivered and Sara was breastfeeding, I left the room to get the equipment. Her husband followed me and told me that he wanted me to *'sew her up and return it to how it was'*. This essentially meant, reinfibulating Sara; I felt unprepared as I was not expecting this. Before I could stop myself, I asked *'why?'* He then explained it was their tradition. Deborah the delivery suite co-ordinator caught my eye as she overheard the conversation.

THEORY: reasons for practising FGM. There are many reasons to justify FGM (see the helpful resources section) and tradition is included (WHO, 2018; Jones and Albert, 2021)

I suddenly became aware that the corridor was not the appropriate place to have this discussion. I then started to consider if I should speak to Sara on her own before speaking to her husband. I questioned whether this also meant there was an increased risk of Sara undergoing reinfibulation outside of hospital care and whether there was also an increased risk of their daughter undergoing the practice of FGM. I knew that my role was to work with families to prevent the perpetuation of FGM for their daughters, but I did not think I would have to have that discussion today, immediately after the birth.

I was conscious that I had to communicate with her husband effectively and sensitively (WHO, 2018) but what does that look like? I realised that Sara may need and want to involve her husband in the decision making (WHO, 2018),

MODEL: personalised care

but I needed to ensure Sara remained the centre of the decision making while taking the opportunity to engage the husband too. I advised the husband to return to the room and I would return very shortly. I quickly spoke to Deborah to affirm my plans of how I would handle the situation. Deborah and I looked again at the labour instructions and birth plan in the maternity records, documented by the FGM specialist midwife. There was a drawing of the deinfibulation and how it should be sutured in the birth plan, as well as documented recording of their discussion about safeguarding future girls from FGM. However, it wasn't clear whether reinfibulation had been discussed with Sara and Karim.

Sara and June were laughing when I entered the room. I felt guilty that I was going to bring a more serious atmosphere into the room. I asked Sara if I could speak to her and her husband about the stitching to be completed. I showed her the diagram that the FGM specialist midwife had drawn and explained how the raw edges would be over-sewn on each side of the vulva region. Sara looked at me as though she knew this. I asked Sara if her husband Karim understood. Sara looked confused. I informed Sara that Karim had instructed me to stitch the raw edges so that it would return to how it was. There was an immediate discussion between Sara and Karim. I could not understand what was said, but Sara's tone of voice appeared emotional. The interpreter explained that Sara was telling her husband about the frequent infections she had experienced and the physical and mental pain when passing urine, menstruating and when they had sexual intercourse. I was surprised at Sara's frankness and realised that it was my own misconception that women could not talk about FGM and its implications with their husbands.

VALUE: professional accountability

EVIDENCE: complications of FGM include vulval and clitoral pain, painful intercourse, pain or difficulty passing urine and menstrual blood, recurrent urinary tract infections, higher renal failure, and risk of keloid scarring and cysts. The increased risks of infections can cause premature birth in the future. Additionally, reinfibulation could increase risks for subsequent labour and birth (WHO, 2018)

VALUES: professional responsibility to do no harm (NMC, 2018) and 're-infibulation is never medically indicated' (WHO, 2018, p 398)

VALUE: safeguarding. Female Genital Mutilation Act 2003 (England, Wales, and Northern Ireland); the Prohibition of Female Genital Mutilation (Scotland) Act 2005 (HM Government, 2020)

VALUE: duty of care. FGM is child abuse (HM Government, 2020)

I had intended to start the conversation explaining my legal and professional responsibilities but reconsidered this when Sara brought up her health issues. I explained that reinfibulation has no health benefits. Karim appeared to be listening and in shock.

I then explained that as a midwife I am bound by my professional responsibilities. I explained that it is illegal to perform FGM in the UK. I also explained that reinfibulation would be categorised as performing FGM. I added that the law includes a prison sentence. I took a breath; I did not want to come across as threatening. Karim put his hands over his face; he appeared to be processing the information. He asked me to explain the deinfibulation diagram and then shared that he did not know what was involved with FGM, only that all women had it done in their community. Karim looked uncomfortable, clammy and the colour drained from his face. I passed him some water.

I questioned whether this was the right time to talk about the risk to their daughter. I had a duty of care to Sara, but I knew I had an obligation to protect their daughter too. I had a loud voice in my head reminding me of the need for 'making every contact count' (Public Health England, 2016). Maybe this would be the only time that Sara and Karim would be in the hospital together. I knew it was important that the husband is an advocate for his daughter. I could not be certain whether their daughter would be at risk.

I began to explain that the request for reinfibulation brings safeguarding concerns because it showed that the husband still retained traditional beliefs around FGM. I then discussed that it is a criminal offence in the UK if parents aid or perform FGM on their daughter, but also the Failure to Protect clause specifies that a mother or father can be prosecuted in the UK for failing to prevent someone else carrying out FGM on their daughter. So even if they are against it themselves, they can be prosecuted. I had already discussed the long-term effects of FGM, but I reinforced that there are also immediate and short-term complications when FGM is first performed. Sara acknowledged the risks and reaffirmed that the FGM specialist midwife had discussed these issues, but Karim was not present. Sara, although tearful, said that she understood that the UK laws were there to protect her baby girl; Karim remained silent. He looked like he was still making sense of all the information. I documented the discussion and that safeguarding needed to be discussed again on the postnatal ward to reinforce all the points discussed.

VALUE: safeguarding: girls may be at risk from any family or extended family members who sometimes perpetuate FGM even against the mother or father's wishes (Ministry of Justice/ Home Office, 2015)

VALUE: safeguarding

EVIDENCE: immediate complications include death, pain, haemorrhage, infection, septicaemia, genital swelling and acute urine retention (WHO, 2018)

Reflections

When Sara arrived on the delivery suite, I was disappointed that the deinfibulation had not been completed during the pregnancy. Although the labour management plan was clearly documented in the maternity records about FGM, I felt anxious about the care in labour and birth. I did not inform Sara that I had never cared for a woman requiring deinfibulation and my anxieties that Sara may have a precipitate labour without an expert available to carry out the deinfibulation. I also recalled that research presented at the last FGM update showed that when deinfibulation is delayed until labour, there is a higher risk of episiotomy, instrumental birth, caesarean section and longer hospital stay (Albert et al, 2015). Listening to Sara, however, and realising the fear connected to the deinfibulation, helped me to empathise more about the risk of flashbacks to the FGM procedure. In future I will assess the woman's mental well-being. I will also have more empathy about personal preferences regarding timing of the deinfibulation as some women prefer the timing to be before marriage, intercourse, during pregnancy or during labour, and that women may need support to adjust to their change of body image following deinfibulation (Evans et al, 2019b). I have also recognised that I have training needs and have organised to spend a day shadowing an FGM specialist midwife.

EVIDENCE: women sometimes present with depression, anxiety, phobias, nightmares and/or post-traumatic stress disorders (WHO, 2018)

Understanding more about assessing the elasticity of the perineal tissue in the second stage of labour, I realised that the same assessment should be completed for FGM types 1, 2 and 4, as well as type 3.

MODEL: the World Health Organization classification of FGM types 1, 2 and 4 (WHO, 2018)

I knew that all disclosures of FGM require a holistic safeguarding risk assessment. Across the UK there are different national legal requirements, as well as local policies and procedures that should be taken into consideration (HM Government, 2020). It was difficult to discuss

VALUE: safeguarding

the safeguarding issues following the birth, but on reflection I feel the timing was right when considering the presence of the interpreter and the husband. These situations must be individually assessed because the timing would not have been right if Sara had experienced a postpartum haemorrhage or the baby needed medical attention. Additional reflections reinforced the importance of men being involved in discussions where possible to help prevent the perpetuation of FGM.

Actions

Reading more about FGM introduced me to the importance of practising trauma-informed care for all women, but particularly with FGM survivors. The principles emphasise the establishment of trust, ensuring safety and yielding control to the patient while minimising discomfort, re-traumatisation and shame (particularly important when performing genital examinations for FGM survivors as these can elicit strong emotional reactions such as flashbacks or vasovagal response) (Rittenberg, 2018).

I explored the timing of deinfibulation within the first stage of labour to guide my future practice. The World Health Organization (2018) and RCOG (2015) FGM guidelines link timing to procedures such as vaginal examinations and catheterisation. The FGM specialist midwives at my organisation advised that deinfibulation should be considered early in the first stage if the vaginal introitus is less than 1 cm and clinical interventions are being considered. However, they also advised there is a risk that the deinfibulation site may bleed and stitching is not advisable until after the birth as the sutures may affect the ability of the tissue to stretch for birth. If labour is progressing well, as in the case of Sara, the deinfibulation can be considered later in the first stage of labour. There is no research evidence available about the timing of deinfibulation in labour. Such knowledge has been gained through experience by healthcare specialists caring for women with FGM. Until more research is completed, I will assess on a case-by-case basis to consider risks.

Questions for reflection and discussion

1. What facilities do you have in your organisation to assess, educate and support women with FGM?

2. What local charities and/or health advocates do you have in your area to signpost women with FGM for extra support?

3. What education and support do you think is needed for men to support women and girls and protect them from FGM?

4. Make a list of the different classifications of FGM and the health implications related to each of them using WHO (2018) and the helpful resources list below.

5. Consider the words you would use to ask a woman if they have experienced FGM. Think about other terms such as female genital cutting and terms used in different languages (HM Government, 2020).

6. What safeguarding and legal responsibilities would you have discussed with Sara and Karim? How can FGM protection orders and health passports (HM Government 2020; GOV UK, 2016) help safeguard females under 18 years old?

Helpful resources

Dahlia Project provides information and support for FGM survivors – www.dahliaproject.org

FGM National Clinical Group (2023) – www.fgmresource.com/videos/fgm-resource-midwives

FORWARD (2023) is a campaign organisation raising awareness about issues facing women and girls – www.forwarduk.org.uk/?gclid=EAIaIQobChMI3ZOsp7Da7wIVCbLtCh1LTQthEAAYAiAAEgKf5_D_BwE

Gov.UK (2022) *Female Genital Mutilation: Resource Pack* – www.gov.uk/government/publications/female-genital-mutilation-resource-pack/female-genital-mutilation-resource-pack

National FGM Centre – http://nationalfgmcentre.org.uk/about-us

NHS (2022) National FGM Support Clinics – www.nhs.uk/conditions/female-genital-mutilation-fgm/national-fgm-support-clinics

NSPCC (2021) Protecting Children from Female Genital Mutilation (FGM) – https://learning.nspcc.org.uk/child-abuse-and-neglect/fgm

References

Albert, J, Bailey, E and Duaso, M (2015) Does the Timing of Deinfibulation for Women with Type 3 Female Genital Mutilation Affect Labour Outcomes? *British Journal of Midwifery*, 23(6): 430–7. [online] Available at: www.magonlinelibrary.com/doi/abs/10.12968/bjom.2015.23.6.430 (accessed 30 December 2022).

Evans, C, Tweheyo, R, McGarry J, Eldridge, J, Albert, J, Nkoyo, V and Higginbottom, G (2019a) Crossing Cultural Divides: A Qualitative Systematic Review of Factors Influencing the Provision of Healthcare Related to Female Genital Mutilation from the Perspective of Health Professionals. *PLOS ONE*, 7(31): 1–32.

Evans, C, Tweheyo, R, McGarry, J, Eldridge, J, Albert, J, Nkoyo, V and Higginbottom, G (2019b) Seeking Culturally Safe Care: A Qualitative Systematic Review of the Healthcare Experiences of Women and Girls Who Have Undergone Female Genital Mutilation/Cutting. *BMJ Open*, 9(5): 1–23.

Female Genital Mutilation Act (2003). [online] Available at: www.legislation.gov.uk/ukpga/2003/31/contents (accessed 14 April 2023).

Gov.UK (2016) Statement Opposing Female Genital Mutilation. [online] Available at: www.gov.uk/government/publications/statement-opposing-female-genital-mutilation (accessed 30 December 2022).

HM Government (2020) Multi-agency Statutory Guidance on Female Genital Mutilation. [online] Available at: www.gov.uk/government/publications/multi-agency-statutory-guidance-on-female-genital-mutilation (accessed 30 December 2022).

Jones, L and Albert, J (2021) Identifying and Responding to Female Genital Mutilation: Reflections from a UK Research–Practice Partnership. In Bradbury-Jones, C and Isham, L (eds) *Understanding Gender-Based Violence* (pp 217–39). Cham: Springer International Publishing.

Ministry of Justice/ Home Office (2015) Serious Crime Act 2015. Factsheet: Overview of Act. [online] Available at: www.gov.uk/government/publications/serious-crime-bill-overarching-documents (accessed 2 January 2023).

NHS Digital (2020) Female Genital Mutilation Datasets. [online] Available at: https://digital.nhs.uk/data-and-information/clinical-audits-and-registries/female-genital-mutilation-datasets (accessed 1 January 2023).

Nursing & Midwifery Council (NMC) (2018) *The Code: Professional Standards of Practice and Behaviour for Nurses, Midwives and Nursing Associates*. London: Nursing & Midwifery Council.

Public Health England (2016) Making Every Contact Count (MECC): Consensus statement. [online] Available at: www.england.nhs.uk/wp-content/uploads/2016/04/making-every-contact-count.pdf (accessed 31 March 2023).

Rittenberg, E (2018) Trauma-Informed Care: Reflections of a Primary Care Doctor in the Week of the Kavanaugh Hearing. *New England Journal of Medicine*, 379(22): 2094–5.

Royal College of Obstetricians and Gynaecologists (RCOG) (2015) *Female Genital Mutilation and its Management*. Green-top Guideline No. 53, July. [online] Available at: www.rcog.org.uk/guidance/browse-all-guidance/green-top-guidelines/female-genital-mutilation-and-its-management-green-top-guideline-no-53 (accessed 30 December 2022).

World Health Organization (WHO) (2018) *Care of Women and Girls Living with Female Genital Mutilation: A Clinical Handbook*. Geneva: World Health Organization. Licence: CC BY-NC-SA 3.0 IGO. [online] Available at: https://apps.who.int/iris/handle/10665/272429 (accessed 30 December 2022).

Case study 9
Rahaf: 'no one puts their children in a boat...'

Katherine Letley and Kenda Crozier

Introduction

The case study introduces some of the professional decisions that occur in the care of asylum seekers. Midwives and health professionals in general work in a system which is free at the point of access for all so the decisions around payment and eligibility do not occur in the UK, unlike in some other health systems. However, consideration of the cost of accessing care and support comes as a shock when we realise that a client has little to live on. The title of the case study is taken from a line in the powerful poem 'Home' by Warsan Shire (2011): *'No one puts their children in a boat unless it is safer than the sea.'*

Appointment 1

I first met Rahaf when she presented for her initial antenatal appointment. She had two small children with her, and it soon became clear that she spoke limited English. I welcomed her into the clinic room and was struck by her physique that suggested she was already quite far along in her pregnancy. Her general practitioner had made me aware that Rahaf was an asylum seeker and that they thought she was booking into antenatal services late but had not provided any information about the need for an interpreter.

VALUE: interprofessional communication

THEORY: establishment of additional care needs

Rahaf was well presented and her children, both under five years old, were neat, appeared nourished, said hello in English and, when invited to, played with the small supply of toys in the corner of the room. I used a telephone interpreting service to take a history from Rahaf. She told me that she did not know she could have antenatal care and had no experience of it in her previous two pregnancies. Both her children had been born in Damascus, Syria.

THEORIES: citizenship and statehood, belonging

THEORIES: displaced people, dispersal, social networks, building social capital

THEORY: individualised care

EVIDENCE: NICE guidelines state that if women have difficulty understanding or speaking English, they should be offered an interpreter to translate. The interpreter should not be a member of the person's family (NICE, 2010)

MODEL: financial cost of healthcare

VALUES: compassion, woman-centredness, confidentiality

EVIDENCE: NICE guidelines (2010) state that to allow sufficient time for interpretation, local antenatal services should offer flexibility in the number and length of appointments, over and above what is outlined in national guidance

She said that the pregnancies were straightforward and she went to hospital to give birth, there had been no problems as far as she knew and her children had no health problems. She told me that her husband had brought her and the children to the UK 18 months ago and they were waiting for a decision on their claim for asylum. They had been in temporary accommodation in Leeds but had recently been moved to Bradford, where they were living in council-provided housing.

I asked her routine questions related to her past medical and obstetric history, her family history and her social and lifestyle circumstances. I spoke to the telephone interpreter who was male; he asked the questions and she answered, albeit, it appeared to me, very briefly. She appeared uncomfortable with some questions about her past pregnancies and medical history. I only had one hour and the appointment ended abruptly because we ran out of time and the children were becoming fractious.

We arranged another appointment for the following week to discuss the birth and a hospital appointment for her to have a scan and an appointment with the phlebotomist to take routine bloods. She said she could walk to the hospital, which was close to her accommodation. I asked her to try to come on her own to our follow-up appointment so I could talk to her more privately and explained I would try to arrange a face-to-face interpreter.

After the first appointment

Reflections

I felt a sense of helplessness about Rahaf's situation. I wished I had had more time and resources to communicate effectively with Rahaf. I felt rushed and stressed about this new complex addition to my caseload. I had no real preparation that I could draw on for managing this additional workload.

I felt unprepared and lacking in understanding about the rights and entitlements of asylum seekers in pregnancy.

I made a note to seek out information and find out from colleagues what I needed to know to provide better support. It is important to remember that I am only one person and part of a larger multi-professional, multi-agency team that can work together to support women with complex needs. I knew that I needed to ensure communication was as easy as possible so booked a female face-to-face interpreter for the next week.

Actions

The next time I was at work, I reviewed Rahaf's records and found out that Rahaf was now approximately 22 weeks' pregnant. I discussed the case with my community mid-wifery team, and a colleague recommended I investigate parenting classes or baby groups to help Rahaf integrate into the community; they made some suggestions for people to contact. I had a look online, and as Bradford has a high demographic of women who are refugees or asylum seekers, I was pleased to see that there was an established mother and baby group at a local community centre.

THEORIES: building social capital, peer support

I did some research and then felt better prepared about how I could support Rahaf. I had not realised that people seeking asylum were only entitled to around £40 per week (correct at the time of going to press); this felt like an exceedingly small amount of money to me. I felt immediately guilty that Rahaf had to pay £4.10 to get the bus to see me at the community clinic and considered that I would arrange some home visits. I had found out that Rahaf could contact Migrant Help, who would inform the Home Office of the pregnancy and add an additional small sum of money onto her weekly asylum payments. I had also identified that Rahaf could apply for a single maternity payment to help with the costs of having a new baby, but that the time when she had to apply was very specific. I made a note in my diary that at Rahaf's 34-week appointment we needed to investigate applying for this additional support. I should be able to find a support worker from the local council who works with people to complete their applications.

MODELS: additional care needs in pregnancy, role of the midwife, multi-agency working

Appointment 2

Rahaf was now 24 weeks' pregnant, feeling fetal movements and said through the female interpreter that she felt much less tired. The interpreter was very professional, and it felt a lot easier to have frank and open conversations with someone face to face; it may also have helped that she was a woman. Despite this, Rahaf still did not make much eye contact with the interpreter. Rahaf seemed more a little more relaxed this time and opened up to me about a previous pregnancy she had experienced while living in a refugee camp in Lebanon. She explained that she had become pregnant unexpectedly and felt trapped by her state of destitution and that she wanted to terminate the pregnancy. She had no access to any health services and a woman in the camp offered to try and help her. She performed an abortion in a non-sterile environment and Rahaf suffered a haemorrhage, which was managed by the *Médecins Sans Frontières* (Doctors without Borders) team on site in the camp. While relaying the story she began to cry. She explained that she did not think she would be able to have another baby due to the complications that had arisen following the procedure. Her explanation of conditions in the camp and her travels to the UK were truly harrowing. Her sense of desperation was very real and she explained that her husband knew little of the detail and he understood that she had 'lost the pregnancy'. She said *'please don't tell my husband... I told him only that I lost the baby'*.

I asked how she felt about this pregnancy and she said she felt it was a blessing and hoped that she would not suffer any consequences from the procedure in the camp. However, when I asked about her mental health and whether she had felt down or depressed in the last month, she said: *'It's hard to be hopeful when we don't know our future.'* She also reported that the night before the scan appointment she had woken from sleep screaming, having a flashback of the procedure in the camp. She said: *'I'm scared about the birth; I don't think I can bear to think about it.'*

MODEL: emergency aid

EVIDENCE: access to family planning and reproductive health services is limited in refugee camps. This is particularly the case in countries such as Lebanon where abortion is illegal. Unsafe abortion is one of the leading causes of maternal morbidity and mortality, particularly in insecure contexts such as a refugee camp (WHO, 2019)

THEORY: loss and grief

VALUE: confidentiality

MODEL: mental health assessment in pregnancy

THEORY: post-traumatic stress disorder symptoms. Signs and symptoms of PTSD include flashbacks and hypervigilance – feeling tense, on guard and being irritable with aggressive outbursts (NICE, 2018)

I was concerned that Rahaf was suffering from post-traumatic stress disorder (PTSD), and after asking some questions about her mental state and using the assessment tools available to midwives, I referred her to the perinatal mental health team. I explained all of this to Rahaf through the interpreter, and as I had more time we were able to take things much slower. Rahaf kept asking what the Home Office would be told, and whether any of her disclosures would impact her asylum claim. I reassured her that nothing she disclosed about her health would impact her ability to achieve refugee status.

Towards the end of the appointment, I explained to Rahaf about the mother and baby group that meets at the local community centre. I explained that the women who attend are from multiple different ethnic backgrounds and that they often have interpreters present. I gently suggested it might be a positive thing to try to go along to in order to build a peer support network to help her combat the isolation she was feeling. Rahaf seemed receptive to this and took the details from me.

After the second appointment

Reflections

I felt overwhelmed by the amount of additional needs Rahaf had. Some of the main barriers to accessing care include communication challenges, isolation, mental health difficulties, the effects of dispersal, housing challenges, professional attitudes and access to health-care (McKnight et al, 2019).

> EVIDENCE: asylum-seeking and refugee women are at higher risk of maternal mortality, pre-term birth and congenital abnormalities alongside an increased risk of mental health issues (Heslehurst et al, 2018)

However, as a midwife I understand how to provide compassionate support to pregnant women, how to provide information that enables them to be part of their own decisions and to monitor the health of mother and fetus. Therefore, although I am daunted by the additional care needs, I can still draw on my skills to provide the universal support that all pregnant women require. Each pregnancy is unique and I can seek out information and support from the multi-agency

> VALUE: compassionate woman-centred care

team around me. My local health-visiting team has some experience in working with asylum seekers and I can arrange a joint appointment with one of them later in the pregnancy.

I felt pleased that I had arranged to use an interpreter as both Rahaf and I had found this much more helpful than the telephone system.

I felt a lot of compassion towards Rahaf for what she and her family had experienced.

I felt overwhelmed by the global events which had forced her to flee, and a bit ashamed about how little I knew about the war in Syria.

Actions

EVIDENCE: asylum-seeking and refugees are more likely to experience mental health issues (Steel et al, 2009)

- I completed a referral to the perinatal mental health team and amended my initial referral for consultant-led care to inform them of the details of Rahaf's termination of pregnancy.

- I arranged a follow-up at 28 weeks as a home visit. I made a note to discuss Rahaf with the health visitor at our next meeting.

Appointment 3: home visit

When visiting Rahaf at home, I met her husband, Abdul, for the first time, who welcomed me into the house. He also had limited English, and this time I had been unable to secure an interpreter so was relying on Language Line. Rahaf appeared more relaxed in her home environment and made an effort to offer me refreshments. The home was very sparse, with one small sofa and a basic table and chairs in the main room. The kitchen was standard and clean, and the children were well behaved, occupied by watching something on Abdul's phone.

We completed the routine antenatal appointment, and all measurements appeared to be within normal parameters. I asked Rahaf whether she had been to the mother and baby group, and she responded positively: her face lit up and she nodded enthusiastically. She showed me on her phone that she was now in a WhatsApp group with other women in the local area who had small children, saying *'friend'* and *'Shakran'*, meaning thank you in Arabic.

EVIDENCE: peer support has the potential to improve physical and mental health outcomes in pregnancy (McLeish and Redshaw, 2015), and this is particularly the case for women seeking asylum (Griswold et al, 2021)

Rahaf had been given a leaflet at the group for an organisation called Doulas Without Borders. I asked Rahaf about it and she nodded and explained via the translator that she had been offered free birth and postnatal support from a doula from this organisation. She was going to explore this more. As her husband had not been at the previous births, she had been helped by other women. With this birth, she wished her husband to remain at home and care for the children. She explained that the doula could help her get to the hospital and provide support during the birth.

I could see from the antenatal notes that Rahaf had a telephone consultation with Lucy, the perinatal mental health specialist midwife, the week before. Rahaf had disclosed that she did not want to have a vaginal delivery due to her fears about vaginal examinations and the potential triggers. Lucy had made a note of this request and emailed the relevant consultant to discuss it further with Rahaf.

MODEL: multi-disciplinary working for additional care in pregnancy

THEORY: trauma-informed care

We finished the appointment, and I left having made plans for Rahaf to see me at the clinic next time. I would also arrange a face-to-face interpreter so we could discuss a few things in more detail. On leaving, I made a note to refer Rahaf to the local baby bank to access some basic things to prepare for the arrival of the new baby.

After the home visit

Reflections

It was upsetting to see the family living in such a sparse home with no toys for the children to play with.

I felt pleased that Rahaf had been in contact with the perinatal mental health team and relieved that plans were being made to ensure Rahaf's intrapartum care was trauma informed. This gives me confidence in the system of multi-professional working that provides a safety net for women with additional needs.

I felt happy that I had been able to signpost Rahaf to a peer support network who would be able to support her and her family long after she had been discharged by the midwifery team.

I had not realised that Rahaf would want any different sort of birth support for her labour. I had assumed her husband would be her birth partner. I questioned my own assumptions and did some research.

I found out about cultural safety packages which could help me better reflect on my own personal bias and stereotypes to provide better care for women from diverse backgrounds. I asked my manager whether we could arrange a session.

Questions for reflection and discussion

1. Consider what you know about the rights of asylum seekers and refugees. How can you take steps to better understand the rights and entitlements to maternity care? How does this link with your understanding of human rights?

2. Consider and explain how individuals in the multi-agency team can work together to identify with Rahaf her care needs and how these can be met in a person-centred, sensitive way.

3. What groups are available in your local area? How could you work with others to identify the social support available?

4. How would you manage your own emotions in this situation?

5. If Rahaf has a diagnosis of post-traumatic stress disorder, depression or anxiety, how will you monitor and support her mental well-being and what plans might be needed for the birth?

6. Have you had cultural competence or cultural safety training within your role? Do you feel confident examining your own personal bias when caring for women from different ethnic backgrounds?

Helpful resources

Doulas Without Borders – www.doulaswithoutborders.com

e-Learning for Healthcare Cultural Competency Package – www.e-lfh.org.uk/programmes/cultural-competence

Maternity Action: Asylum Seekers – Financial Support and Housing – https://maternityaction.org.uk/advice/asylum-seekers-financial-support-and-housing

Maternity Action: Information-sharing between the NHS and Home Office– https://maternityaction.org.uk/advice/information-sharing-between-the-home-office-and-the-nhs

Maternity Stream of Sanctuary Resource Pack – https://cdn.cityofsanctuary.org/uploads/sites/45/2022/11/MATERNITY-RESOURCE-PACK-24-10-22-ammended-links.pdf

Médecins Sans Frontières (Doctors without Borders) – www.msf.org

Migrant Help – www.migranthelpuk.org/pages/category/asylum

NHS England: *Good Practice Guide for Implementation of Trauma-informed Care in the Perinatal Period* – www.england.nhs.uk/wp-content/uploads/2021/02/BBS-TIC-V8.pdf

Refugee Council: *Maternity Care in the UK for Women on Asylum Support* – https://media.refugeecouncil.org.uk/wp-content/uploads/2021/10/29174133/Maternity-care-in-the-UK-for-women-on-asylum-support-read-version_July_2021.pdf

Royal College of Midwives: *Caring for Vulnerable Migrant Women* – www.rcm.org.uk/media/5280/caring-for-vulnerable-migrant-women-2020-125x85mm_14.pdf

Royal College of Obstetricians and Gynaecologists: *Considering a Caesarean Birth Patient Information Leaflet* – www.rcog.org.uk/for-the-public/browse-all-patient-information-leaflets/choosing-to-have-a-caesarean-section

UK Government Guidance, NHS Entitlements: Migrant Health Guide – www.gov.uk/guidance/nhs-entitlements-migrant-health-guide

References

Griswold, K, Vest, B, Lynch-Jiles, A, Sawch, D, Kolesnikova, K, Byimana, L and Kefi, P (2021) 'I Just Need to Be with My Family': Resettlement Experiences of Asylum Seeker and Refugee Survivors of Torture. *Globalization and Health*, 17: 27.

Heslehurst, N, Brown, H, Pemu, A, Coleman, H and Rankin, J (2018) Perinatal Health Outcomes and Care Amongst Asylum Seekers and Refugees: A Systematic Review of Systematic Reviews. *BMC Medicine*, 16: 89.

McKnight, P, Goodwin, L and Kenyon, S (2019) A Systematic Review of Asylum-Seeking Women's Views and Experiences of UK Maternity Care. *Midwifery*, 77: 16–23.

McLeish, J and Redshaw, M (2015) Peer Support during Pregnancy and Early Parenthood: A Qualitative Study of Models and Perceptions. *BMC Pregnancy and Childbirth*, 15: 257.

National Institute for Health and Care Excellence (NICE) (2010) Pregnancy and Complex Social Factors: A Model for Service Provision for Pregnant Women with Complex Social Factors. [online] Available at: www.nice.org.uk/guidance/CG110/chapter/1-Guidance#pregnant-women-who-are-recent-migrants-asylum-seekers-or-refugees-or-who-have-difficulty-reading (accessed 9 March 2023).

National Institute for Health and Care Excellence (NICE) (2018) Post-Traumatic Stress Disorder. [online] Available at: www.nice.org.uk/guidance/ng116 (accessed 9 March 2023).

Shire, W (2011) *Teaching My Mother How to Give Birth*. London: Flipped Eye Publishing Limited.

Steel, Z, Chey, T, Silove, D, Marnane, C, Bryant, R and van Ommeren, M (2009) Association of Torture and Other Potentially Traumatic Events with Mental Health Outcomes Among Populations Exposed to Mass Conflict and Displacement: A Systematic Review and Meta-analysis. *JAMA*, 302: 537–49.

World Health Organization (WHO) (2019) *Trends in Maternal Mortality 2000 to 2017*. [online] Available at: www.who.int/publications/i/item/9789241516488 (accessed 9 March 2023).

Case study 10
Oli: hello my name is... my pronouns are...

Katherine Letley and Kenda Crozier

Introduction

This case study highlights the way in which transgender people experience maternity care. In supporting the individual, midwives are sometimes in a position where they are trying to deal with a system which is not inclusive. This leads to dilemmas around challenging the attitudes and behaviours of others and supporting decision making through individualised care planning.

The initial midwife consultation

When I called 'Olivia' from the midwifery clinic waiting room, a man got up from his chair and walked towards me. I looked behind him to see if the newly pregnant woman was somehow behind him. He greeted me saying he was my patient – *'please don't look so surprised'* – that he would rather be called Oli and that his pronouns are he and him. He stated that the GP surgery had been told to change his name from Olivia to Oli on file but that they often still got it wrong. I apologised, introduced myself, gave my pronouns as she and her and invited Oli into the clinic room. Oli informed me that he is a 32 year-old transgender man.

I have had some experience in supporting couples and parents from the Lesbian, Gay, Bisexual, Trans, Queer or Questioning and others (LGBTQ+) community but was a bit fazed by this meeting. As I began to look at the initial consultation record that I was going to complete with Oli, I was struck by how often it referenced *'the woman'* or *'mother'*. Even the term *'maternity'* seemed to be inappropriate. I explained to Oli that the documentation was not suited to a transgender person experiencing a pregnancy, but it was what we had to work with at this time. I wondered if it was

THEORY: individualised care, person-centred care

VALUES: compassion, inclusion and respect (the Code, NMC, 2018)

EVIDENCE: respectful care recognises and affirms the gender identity of the pregnant person and normalises the experience of carrying a pregnancy while trans or non-binary (Green and Riddington, 2020, p 7)

EVIDENCE: use of language in pregnancy

THEORY: instituitional erasure:
this could be viewed as
institutional erasure, which is
when signs and documents erase
the trans person from discourse
surrounding pregnancy and birth
(Botelle et al, 2021)

THEORY: conflict between
dominant social norms and
identity (Botelle et al, 2021)

possible to find any alternatives, though I thought it unlikely.

I am mindful that midwives should treat every pregnancy as unique and offer individualised care as far as we can, but the reality is that the forms, documents and information tend to be geared towards the needs of the system.

Instead of starting with the form I began with my usual question: '*How do you feel about being pregnant?*' Oli then told me his story of transition and his desire for a baby. As he entered his 30s he felt that he wanted to explore whether he would be able to conceive following years of being medicated with testosterone. He spent a lot of time researching his options, stopped taking the testosterone and eventually became pregnant via a sperm donor. I assumed he had received in vitro fertilisation (IVF) treatment, but he informed me that he had inseminated at home with sperm bought online to save on costs. He was very well informed and explained that the sperm bank ensured it had been thoroughly screened. He said that he felt excited and slightly terrified all at the same time when he realised he was pregnant. This is a reaction I have heard often from people who have undergone IVF or fertility treatment. I told Oli that because his method of conception was artificial, the NHS Trust guidelines stated I needed to refer him for consultant-led care in the first instance. Oli accepted the need to see a consultant but asked if this meant he would have to tell his story again to yet another professional.

EVIDENCE: NICE guidelines
do not state that assisted
conception is a reason for
consultant-led review; however,
individual hospital guidance
may vary

I asked about whether he had a partner or social support network as he had come to the appointment on his own. Oli explained that he is currently single but has a supportive mother and sister who he lives with. Although he had many cisgendered friends who had children, his only network with other trans parents was online.

THEORY: marginalisation. Social
support is a crucial element in
transition to parenting and can
be a protective factor against
postnatal depression

We talked through the questions on the form. I asked about his previous medical history other than his gender transition as he had already explained that. He disclosed episodes of depression as a teenager that manifested in self-harm. He had been prescribed anti-depressant medication, which he had taken for three years. He stopped taking this medication once his gender transition was underway and he was supported in doing so. I asked the questions about his mental well-being and let him know that if he was experiencing any symptoms of anxiety or low mood, he could ask for help at any point in the pregnancy.

When making my way through the paperwork, I hesitated over the questions regarding family history. Although Oli had conceived using his own egg, the sperm was from an unknown donor. Oli was unable to offer any information regarding the sperm donor and his family history. Oli looked a bit upset about this and asked whether it would be a problem. Again, I hesitated, but then reassured Oli that with a fair number of pregnancies very little is known about the entire family history.

When asking about previous surgeries, Oli disclosed he had 'top surgery' done two years ago. He was also on testosterone up until six months ago when he stopped to allow his body to conceive.

I asked Oli when he last had a smear test done. Oli was confused and stated he had never been invited for a smear test. I checked the GP records and, as his gender had been changed to 'male' when he was 19, he had not received his invitation when he turned 25. Oli was very frustrated about this and reported often receiving poor care from the GP surgery, who consistently misgendered him, called him by his old name and had now 'messed this up' and impacted his access to screening for cervical cancer. I apologised on behalf of the surgery and made a note that Oli should be invited for a smear once he was postnatal.

I began to discuss antenatal classes with Oli. I was conscious that I could not signpost Oli to any classes which would not consistently use the terms 'mother' and 'woman' and which might be specific to his needs as a transgender person. I decided to look this up once Oli had gone so

EVIDENCE: 'When asking sensitive questions, for example regarding hormone therapy or surgical history, professionals should explain why this information is relevant, and ensure enquiries are clinically meaningful rather than motivated by curiosity' (Green and Riddington, 2020, p 10)

EVIDENCE: dysphoria, isolation and exclusion are factors that may impact on perinatal mental health (Greenfield and Darwin, 2020)

MODEL: UK Human Fertilisation and Embryology Guidelines state the minimum screening requirements for sperm donors (HFEA.gov.uk)

EVIDENCE: Hoffkling et al (2017) suggest that as testosterone is a teratogen it should be stopped prior to conception and during pregnancy

EVIDENCE: Silver (2022) suggests that people with cervixes registered as male may be missed in screening for cervical cancer. People who are transgender often have difficult experiences accessing healthcare as the system is not designed to meet their needs. This can affect how individuals come to perceive and trust healthcare institutions (Silver, 2022)

THEORY: individualised care

I could signpost him to something more appropriate at his next appointment.

I raised *'place of birth'* options tentatively as I do with all pregnant people at the initial consultation, making it clear that the decision of where to give birth does not need to be taken immediately and we could discuss this again at other appointments. I explained that the local hospital has a midwife-led birthing unit and a consultant-led unit. There is also the choice of a home birth or a separate standalone midwife-led unit, which is further away. He said he was glad I had raised this as his sister and mother had advised him to ask for a caesarean section so that he could have 'control' over everything that is happening. He was unsure about it and did not want to have to make the decision now. I wondered aloud if he was concerned about anything relating to giving birth. He said that his feelings are complicated: on the one hand he would like to have a relaxed, very private experience at home, but at the same time was concerned about anything going wrong and so the idea of being in hospital surrounded by *'machines that go beep'* might be reassuring. He had viewed various videos on social media of water births but was not sure if that was for him. I suggested this may be something he would like to discuss at his appointment with the obstetric consultant.

EVIDENCE: NICE guidance on caesarean birth: NICE guideline NG192 (2014), recommendation 1.3.3 and quality statements 2, 3 and 4; RCOG (2022). Most doctors will not recommend elective caesarean section unless it is for medical reasons (RCOG, 2022)

VALUE: every individual has the right to make decisions about the circumstances in which they give birth (Article 8, European Convention on Human Rights, Council of Europe, 1952)

I asked him about infant feeding choices, and he sighed and said *'Can we come back to that another day? I know the benefits of breastfeeding, but I am not sure if I can do that following my surgery'*. As the appointment ended, I explained that I would be his named midwife for the pregnancy and as far as possible I would arrange for him to see me at all the subsequent appointments. I gave him my contact details for any questions he might have and talked him through the schedule of appointments. As I showed him out, I felt the need to apologise for the documents and the language which may not feel right to him. I also said: *'I want to work with you and for you to feel comfortable so if I slip up with language or say the wrong thing, please help me and let me know. I will be guided by you.'*

MODEL: continuity of care

After the consultation

Reflections

When I saw Oli in the waiting room, I thought he was in the wrong place or was a birth partner, not the pregnant person awaiting my care. I felt out of my depth, desperately not wanting to say the wrong thing, cause offence or make him feel uncomfortable. I was worried that my ignorance and that of my colleagues and the system at large would reduce Oli's willingness to engage and impact on his right to access services. I later read that 32 per cent of trans people have experienced some form of unequal treatment from healthcare staff (Stonewall, 2018) and I really did not want this to happen to Oli.

> EVIDENCE: protected characteristics, Equality Act 2010

In reflecting on this experience, I thought of other areas where I have lacked knowledge and how I have managed to develop understanding of an unfamiliar topic or situation. I usually ask the person to explain what they understand about their health, the medication they are receiving and any support needs they know about. My approach has always been to seek out knowledge, through the Trust Library and my professional organisation, and to liaise with other professionals, exchanging information to provide best care. By working in this partnership approach and listening carefully to the person at the centre of care, I can navigate through the needs of the individual, taking account of their wishes.

It was important that I developed an understanding of best practice so I accessed literature (Botelle et al, 2021; Silver, 2022) to identify what we could do differently. I planned to take the information to the midwifery team and to suggest the need for a local guideline so that we could ensure that pathways of care for pregnant trans people would be equitable and staff would have a point of information.

Actions

The NHS Trust I work for does not have any guidance related to caring for LGBTQ+ people during pregnancy, so I did some research after the appointment and learnt about the guidelines produced by the Brighton and Sussex University Hospital (BSUH), which have been made freely available to share in order to support best practice. Through their website I was able to download pronoun stickers, gender inclusion posters and a sheet about language preferences for Oli to include in his notes. I also downloaded information about perinatal care for trans and non-binary people and a patient information leaflet.

I shared everything I had learned at our next community midwives meeting, as I wanted each staff member to be aware of the specific care Oli needed. I felt it was important to emphasise that the experience of being misgendered or 'dead-named' by a health professional can be catastrophic for the building of a trusting relationship (Silver, 2022). I was struck that actually, as midwives, we are used to changing our language to make service users more comfortable. We often use the word 'surge' rather than contraction for people who hypnobirth, so why should this language shift be any different? I stressed to my colleagues that we already had the necessary skills to change language and individualise care; it was just a matter of being better informed and using the terms Oli preferred. This topic created a good deal of discussion and not everyone agreed with my views about altering documents or providing posters. The discussion became emotive and there was reference to social media discussions on many other trans issues. Some colleagues were offended and declared that biology enabled women to give birth and therefore all birthing people are women biologically. The meeting ended with no consensus, and I sought support from the team leader to take the discussion to the community leadership team and suggest a pathway for trans people to avoid confusion.

THEORY: individualised care, person-centred care

I researched antenatal education that was specific for people like Oli. I came across a website called 'The Queer Parenting Partnership', which offers antenatal and postnatal education and support. I made a note of the website to suggest to Oli when I next saw him.

While researching additional resources for trans people during pregnancy, I came across some blogs about dressing with a baby bump as someone who identifies as male. This had not even crossed my mind as something Oli might be worrying about. However, it was clear that by feeling more comfortable in his clothes, Oli may be less likely to experience gender dysphoria in relation to his changing body while pregnant. I made a note to sensitively bring this up with Oli during his next appointment, so he knew that there were resources out there to help him feel comfortable in his changing body.

THEORY: gender dysphoria

Questions for reflection and discussion

1. How are guidelines developed in your hospital and how are service users involved?

2. Consider involving yourself in providing input to create inclusive guidelines. How could you go about doing this?

3. Reflect on your own experiences of supporting parents from the LGBTQ+ community and consider how you might support Oli.

4. Consider societal views and opinions surrounding language such as 'birthing person' or 'chest feeding'. How are your personal views shaped? How can personal views influence the care we provide?

5. In the NMC (2019) Standards of Proficiency for Midwives, Standard 1.8 states 'demonstrate an understanding of an ability to challenge discriminatory behaviour'. Consider how you might challenge the negative attitudes and behaviour of colleagues which may be discriminatory.

6. Use some of the resources below, such as Green and Riddington (2020) and the queer parenting partnership resource, to help you compile a list of topics for discussion when you begin to co-create a plan of care for Oli.

Helpful resources

Birth for Every Body – www.birthforeverybody.org. This organisation promotes inclusive culturally sensitive information to support all families.

Birthrights Factsheet: *Your Right to a Caesarean Birth* – www.birthrights.org.uk/factsheets/right-to-a-c-section

Brighton and Sussex University Hospitals NHS Trust: NHS Guidelines and Resources. *Support for Trans and Non-binary People During Pregnancy, Birth and the Postnatal Period* – www.bsuh.nhs.uk/wp-content/uploads/sites/5/2016/09/Support-for-trans-and-non-binary-people-during-pregnancy-birth-and-the-postnatal-period.pdf

La Leche League – Infant feeding support for transgender and non-binary parents – www.laleche.org.uk/support-transgender-non-binary-parents

SEAHORSE – https://Seahorsefilm.com

Support organisations – All About Trans – https://onroadmedia.org.uk/work/all-about-trans

The Queer Parenting Partnership – www.parentingqueer.co.uk

Trans fertility resources – https://transfertility.co/resources

References

Botelle, R, Connolly, D, Walker, S and Bewley, S (2021) Contemporary and Future Transmasculine Pregnancy and Postnatal Care in the UK. *The Practising Midwife*, 24(5): 8–13.

Council of Europe (1952) *Article 8, European Convention on Human Rights.* Strasbourg: Directorate of Information.

Green, H and Riddington, A (2020) *Perinatal Care for Trans and Non-Binary People.* Clinical Guideline MP005. [online] Available at: www.bsuh.nhs.uk/maternity/wp-content/uploads/sites/7/2021/01/MP005-Perinatal-Care-for-Trans-and-Non-Binary-People.pdf (accessed 9 March 2023).

Greenfield, M and Darwin, Z (2020) Trans and Non-binary Pregnancy, Traumatic Birth and Perinatal Mental Health: A Scoping Review. *International Journal of Transgender Health*, 22: 203–16.

Hoffkling, A Obedin-Maliver, J and Sevelius, J (2017) From Erasure to Opportunity: A Qualitative Study of the Experiences of Transgender Men around Pregnancy and Recommendations for Providers. *BMC Pregnancy and Childbirth*, 17: 332.

National Institute for Health and Care Excellence (NICE) (2014) *Antenatal and Postnatal Mental Health: Clinical Management and Service Guidance.* [online] Available at: www.nice.org.uk/guidance/cg192/resources/antenatal-and-postnatal-mental-health-clinical-management-and-service-guidance-pdf-35109869806789 (accessed 9 March 2023).

Nursing & Midwifery Council (NMC) (2018) *The Code: Professional Standards of Practice and Behaviour for Nurses, Midwives and Nursing Associates.* London: Nursing & Midwifery Council.

Nursing & Midwifery Council (NMC) (2019) *Standards of Proficiency for Midwives.* [online] Available at: www.nmc.org.uk/globalassets/sitedocuments/standards/standards-of-proficiency-for-midwives.pdf (accessed 23 January 2023)

Royal College of Obstetricians and Gynaecologists (RCOG) (2022) *Considering a Caesarean Birth Patient Information Leaflet*. [online] Available at: www.rcog.org.uk/for-the-public/browse-all-patient-information-leaflets/choosing-to-have-a-caesarean-section (accessed 9 March 2023).

Silver, A (2022) *Supporting Queer Birth: A Book for Birth Professionals and Parents*. London: Jessica Kingsley.

Stonewall (2018) *LGBT in Britain – Health*. [online] Available at: www.stonewall.org.uk/lgbt-britain-health (accessed 9 March 2023).

Case study 11
Lucy: pregnant in a pandemic

Melanie Applegate and Kirstin Pope

Introduction

This case study describes some of the dilemmas encountered by midwives in the context of supporting birth during the Covid-19 pandemic. The restrictions placed by hospitals to contain and manage the infection risks meant that partners were not allowed to be present during appointments and admissions unless in established labour. However, some hospital trusts in areas of high Covid rates only allowed partners to be present when birth was imminent. Midwives work with families and this case highlights some of the ways in which midwives had to work differently, creating a sense of discomfort for them and their clients in the face of many restrictions.

My baby is not moving as much as before and I have Covid-19

Lucy contacted the maternity assessment unit (MAU), reporting she has experienced reduced movements for the past 24 hours and that she is Covid positive. I am one of the two midwives working within the MAU and take some more details from her. This is her second pregnancy, and from reading the electronic maternity records all has been well up to this point of 32 weeks' gestation. Lucy has delayed contacting the unit for advice because of her worries and anxieties about having to attend the hospital with her Covid-positive status and knowing that it is likely her partner will not be able to attend with her.

I advise Lucy that she does need to come to the hospital and although her partner will not be able to come into the hospital with her due to the Covid restrictions, he can be present via video call during her consultations. This provides Lucy with the reassurance to attend and relieves some of her anxieties.

Following the telephone call to the maternity assessment unit

Prior to Lucy's arrival, I discuss Lucy's history and formulate a plan of care with the midwifery co-ordinator and obstetric on-call team. In accordance with the guidance on infection control, I prepare a side room, which is sealed off from the rest of the unit. I collect all the equipment which I require. This will ensure that I will not need to exit the room for any equipment, therefore reducing the potential transmission of the Covid-19 virus to others. The equipment includes a phone so that a review by the obstetric team can take place when required.

EVIDENCE: NHS England (2020). The guidance was produced and updated during the pandemic to ensure that infection risks were minimised in hospital and healthcare settings

There are different types of risk assessment, including risk of the mother's condition deteriorating due to the infection. There is also a risk to the baby, although research has shown some immunity in babies whose mothers were infected with Covid-19. However, with a communicable disease such as Covid-19 there is also a need to use containment measures to reduce the risk of infection spread. Significant adjustments have been made to the healthcare delivery system to prevent infection (Schmitt et al, 2021). These adjustments included barrier nursing to limit the exposure to staff and other service users (wearing personal protective equipment (PPE)), and partners not able to accompany women into the Trust other than when they were in established labour to reduce the possibility of transmission of Covid-19 in accordance with the national lockdown that was currently in place. Routine Covid screening was also conducted on all service users attending the hospital to identify their Covid status – this form of assessment would enable staff to implement the appropriate Covid pathway of care.

EVIDENCE: Karavadra et al (2020). This study consisted of 1,451 women who were either pregnant in May 2020 or had delivered their baby within the Covid-19 pandemic. These women were from a variety of areas across the UK and were asked to complete an online questionnaire with the aim of investigating the preconceptions of pregnant women about Covid-19 and their healthcare expectations

MODEL: public health infection control

These assessments allow me to provide a high standard of care while minimising my own exposure. I formulate plans of care in collaboration with the consultant obstetrician and the midwifery co-ordinator, based on the possible outcomes of the assessment I will undertake. I don the correct PPE, comprising a surgical gown, two pairs of surgical gloves, theatre hat, FFP3 face mask and visor prior to leaving the unit and meeting Lucy in the hospital car park. I am awaiting a phone call from her or her partner to tell me that she has arrived at the hospital, and then I will make my way to meet her. Lucy is aware that that she is required to wear a face mask.

MODEL: infection control, NHS England (2020)

Arrival at hospital

On Lucy's arrival at the hospital, I meet her in the car park wearing full PPE. Lucy immediately makes her apologies for having to come to the hospital knowing that she is Covid positive. When I take Lucy into the hospital and to the MAU, I am conscious that I am dressed in full PPE and therefore other members of staff who we pass on our way to the maternity unit will be aware of Lucy's Covid-positive status. On arrival at the MAU, we go into a side room which is sealed off from the rest of the department. I advise Lucy of the assessment that I will undertake and that the obstetric team will be contacted to review the assessment. This will be conducted via phone as per the current Covid pandemic guidelines. I advise Lucy that her partner is welcome to be on the phone throughout the assessment and both Lucy and her partner are encouraged to ask any questions or raise any concerns that they have.

VALUE: communication. Rypkema (2019) states that midwives need a plethora of effective communication tools and the necessary skills to use them in a variety of situations. Effective communication is not only for use with the pregnant woman but also with her partner and extended family

I relayed my findings to the obstetric team via phone. After auscultating the fetal heartbeat, I commence a Dawes Redman Cardiotography (CTG), which will enable a computerised analysis of the trace and thus minimise the need for other staff to attend Lucy's review.

As the CTG recording is deemed normal and Lucy begins to feel fetal movements during the monitoring, I can discharge Lucy home. It is of paramount importance that I make sure that Lucy is feeling reassured by the findings and knows that she must contact us immediately if she experiences reduced movements again in the future and the rationale behind this.

EVIDENCE: Green-top guidance for reduced fetal movements, RCOG (Royal College of Obstetricians and Gynaecologists) (2011)

I want to be able to provide advice for both Lucy and her partner so that they both feel included in the discussion regarding their baby's well-being. I am aware Lucy's partner

VALUES: compassion, inclusion and respect (the Code, NMC, 2018; Brigante et al, 2022). Midwives found that protective clothing made personal contact with women more difficult because the masks and goggles did not allow facial expressions and their charges could not recognise a 'comforting smile'. Communication in the 'new normal' had to be readjusted accordingly (Schmitt et al, 2021, p 18)

is incredibly concerned and worried. It has been a distressing event for them both. This has been further exacerbated by not being able to attend in person. I do not want this to affect the bonding process for Lucy's partner and feel I need to spend extra time explaining the situation to them both, possibly needing to repeat myself due to Lucy's partner being on the phone and having numerous communication barriers due to my PPE.

Reflections

Due to the pandemic and enforcement of lockdown, members of the public were not allowed within the hospital but it would have been evident to staff that I was meeting a patient who had a Covid-positive status because I was wearing full PPE. We did not wear full PPE if the status was Covid negative. This would never have compromised any care that I provided but was another challenge when carrying out my professional duties and it felt quite overwhelming.

VALUE: communication

EVIDENCE: 'Pregnant women showed high levels of anxiety and depression symptomatology. Fear of contagion and concerns regarding the health of the fetus were identified as the main variables related to psychological distress' (Campos-Garzón et al, 2021, p 1). 'Reducing stress and psychopathological symptoms during pregnancy can also promote the health of the fetus' (Campos-Garzón et al, 2021, p 13)

It saddened me that Lucy felt that she had to make apologies for coming to the hospital. No birthing person should ever feel the need to apologise for seeking help or advice from their midwifery team.

I was also extremely conscious of the potential psychological impact that this could have on Lucy during the rest of her pregnancy and beyond.

In the side room I provided Lucy with routine care and carried out the observations as per the guidelines for reduced fetal movement. Lucy would be putting all her trust in me as I was the only member of staff who she would have face-to-face contact with. This created additional pressure while auscultating the fetal heart. If I could not auscultate a heartbeat, an ultrasound scan would be required to confirm that a heartbeat was either present or not. As I am not trained to perform an ultrasound scan, I would have needed to contact one of the obstetric team, potentially causing further delay and stress for both Lucy,

Lucy's partner (who was present by video call) and myself. The relief that I felt was indescribable upon locating a fetal heartbeat and the relief in Lucy's eyes was immense. I hoped that Lucy felt the empathy I was feeling towards her as a midwife. In the midwifery profession we constantly use non-verbal communication and body language, enabling us to build a rapport with the birthing people we care for. While I understood the rationale for wearing full PPE, it did concern me that this would be detrimental to building that relationship.

I was worried that my own anxieties with having to work in what felt like total isolation from my colleagues and the obstetric team would hinder portraying that caring effect to Lucy. Even though I knew that I could contact my colleagues at any point by phone it still felt like I was very much working in isolation during this scenario. If I had not been able to locate a fetal heartbeat, even though I knew that I could phone for assistance, somehow the extra delay before a colleague would have been able to attend made me feel extremely anxious. I also found it difficult and frustrating that Lucy's partner was not allowed to be physically present and provide Lucy with the emotional support she needed.

EVIDENCE: Sanders and Blaylock (2021) found that women regarded the restrictions on care in labour to be particularly distressing. Hospitals imposed strict infection control measures that caused anxiety both during and after the birth that women described as traumatising

As a senior midwife with many previous experiences of women attending the MAU reporting reduced fetal movements beyond 24 hours resulting in a poor outcome, my immediate feelings were of concern. I did not want to cause any undue alarm; therefore, I made sure I used compassionate communication skills while trying to make sure that Lucy understood the importance of attending the MAU.

VALUES: empathy/compassion

I was empathetic towards Lucy's situation and her rationale for her delay in contacting the MAU. Covid-19 guidance was continually changing not only for healthcare professionals but for the public in general. I was very much aware that birthing people were reluctant to make contact when they had any concerns regarding their pregnancies.

EVIDENCE: significant insight into the perceived barriers to seeking healthcare during this pandemic in a qualitative study included 'not wanting to bother anyone', 'lack of wider support from allied healthcare workers' and the influence of the media. Other concerns included the use of virtual clinics antenatally and their acceptability to patients, the presence of birthing partners, and the way in which information is communicated about rapidly changing and evolving services (Karavadra et al, 2020)

During those last three months, life had changed dramatically at a rapid pace with a national lockdown in force due to the pandemic. The measures included social distancing, mask wearing and limited time outside. The unknown of how this could impact on our health was frightening and many birthing people I was caring for were visibly scared and anxious. Staff were also feeling extremely anxious about this new and unknown territory while trying to always remain professional in their provision of care. I was finding it quite difficult to deal with my own thoughts and anxieties with the knowledge that Lucy was Covid-19 positive. However, I worked hard to put those fears aside to remain the same professional and unbiased midwife.

VALUE: duty of care

With the current situation and restrictions in place, the policy was that I would see Lucy within the assessment unit by myself with no other health professionals present and would provide their consultation via telephone. I found this situation extremely tough. What would have always been a difficult aspect of care during pre-pandemic times was exacerbated due to the altered care pathways and the wearing of PPE.

Lucy delayed seeking care due to her worries and concerns not only because of her reduced fetal movements and the anxiety surrounding this, but also because of her Covid-19 status and navigating the implementation of altered care pathways, which included the wearing of PPE and the reality that her partner would be unable to attend alongside her. I gave Lucy and her partner a high standard of care to the best of my ability despite these barriers. This situation made me question how many pregnant people are not seeking help in a timely manner due to either having Covid-19 or the fear of contracting Covid-19 by leaving their homes.

EVIDENCE: uncertainty about the pandemic also raised fears of infection and spreading the virus. Together, these increased anxiety and stress in maternity staff. Fear of infection was not unfounded and was the greatest reason for higher anxiety (Schmitt et al, 2021). 'More than 85% of health personnel feared for their own health and 89% had increased stress' (Rao et al, 2021)

Having to step outside of my comfort zone was proving to be extraordinarily difficult. I had become accustomed to the habits and patterns of normal ways of working and it was very evident that I was having to try and navigate my own anxieties with regard to this new way of working in an environment that I had always felt very safe and comfortable in. In addition, I also had the extra worry of contracting Covid-19 myself and the risk of taking it home to my own family.

Actions

Prior to Lucy leaving the unit, I reiterated the importance of contacting us at any time if she had any further concerns or questions without delay and she said that she felt reassured today. I did feel confident that Lucy would not hesitate to contact us again if she had any further concerns or questions due to the individualised holistic care we provided during this unprecedented time.

VALUE: holistic care

Questions for reflection and discussion

1. What would be the potential psychological impact of experiencing a pregnancy during the Covid-19 pandemic for Lucy and her partner?

2. Consider and explain Lucy's human rights and how they may have been affected in this situation.

3. How did staff in this situation try to ameliorate the effects of separation from her partner and was there more that could have been done?

4. How can midwives ensure that women with concerns are able to seek advice and guidance in a timely way?

5. Consider and discuss the impact the Covid-19 pandemic had on the midwife. What coping strategies did they accumulate from this?

6. How would you manage your own emotions and what coping strategies would you put in place?

Helpful resources

The Royal College of Nursing provides a helpful guide to duty of care – www.rcn.org.uk/Get-Help/RCN-advice/duty-of-care

UN resources on Covid-19 – www.un.org/en/coronavirus

References

Brigante, L, Morellie, A, Jokinen, M, Plachcinski, R and Rowe, R (2022) Impact of the COVID-19 Pandemic on Midwifery-Led Service Provision in the United Kingdom in 2020–21: Findings of Three National Surveys. *Midwifery*, 112: 103390.

Campos-Garzón, C, Riquelme-Gallego, B, de la Torre-Luque, A and Caparrós-González, R A (2021) Psychological Impact of the COVID-19 Pandemic on Pregnant Women: A Scoping Review. *Behavioral Science (Basel)*, 11(12): 181.

Karavadra, B, Stockl, A, Prosser-Snelling, E, Simpson, P and Morris, E (2020) Women's Perceptions of COVID-19 and Their Healthcare Experiences: A Qualitative Thematic Analysis of a National Survey of Pregnant Women in the United Kingdom. *BMC Pregnancy and Childbirth*, 20: 600.

NHS England (2020) *Specialty Guides for Patient Management During the Coronavirus Pandemic: Clinical Guide for the Temporary Reorganisation of Intrapartum Maternity Care During the Coronavirus Pandemic*. 9 April. Version 1. [online]. Available at: https://madeinheene.hee.nhs.uk/Portals/0/Clinical%20guide%20for%20the%20temporary%20reorganisation%20of%20intrapartum%20maternity%20care.pdf (accessed 31 March 2023).

Nursing & Midwifery Council (NMC) (2018) *The Code: Professional Standards of Practice and Behaviour for Nurses, Midwives and Nursing Associates*. London: Nursing & Midwifery Council.

Rao, S P N et al (on behalf of the COVID-19 Small and Sick Newborn Care Collaborative Group) (2021) Small and Sick Newborn Care during the COVID-19 Pandemic: Global Survey and Thematic Analysis of Healthcare Providers' Voices and Experiences. *BMJ Global Health*, 6(3).

Royal College of Obstetricians and Gynaecologists (RCOG) (2011) *Reduced Fetal Movements*. RCOG Green-top Guideline No. 57. [online] Available at: www.rcog.org.uk/media/2gxndsd3/gtg_57.pdf (accessed 9 March 2023).

Rypkema, T (2019) Effective Communication. In Hutton, E, Murray-Davis, B, Kaufamn, K, Carty, E and Buter, M (eds) *Comprehensive Midwifery: The Role of the Midwife in Health Care Practice, Education, and Research*. [online] Available at: https://ecampusontario.pressbooks.pub/cmroleofmidwifery/ (accessed 9 March 2023).

Sanders, J and Blaylock, R (2021) 'Anxious and traumatised': Users' Experiences of Maternity Care in the UK During the COVID-19 Pandemic. *Midwifery*, 102: 103069.

Schmitt, N, Mattern, E, Cignacco, E, Seliger, G, Konig-Bachmann, M, Striebich, S and Ayerle, G M (2021) Effects of the Covid-19 Pandemic on Maternity Staff in 2020 – a Scoping Review. *BMC Health Service Research*, 21: 1364.

Case study 12
Drew: escaping the clique

Helen Meehan and Melanie Applegate

Introduction

Midwifery is a caring profession and yet it is acknowledged and documented that it has an issue with bullying (Bharj and Marshall, 2019). Bullying is defined by ACAS (2021) as *'unwanted behaviour from a person or group that is either offensive, intimidating, malicious or insulting, or an abuse or misuse of power that undermines, humiliates or causes physical or emotional harm to someone'*. While the profession has sought solutions, they do not appear to be easily implemented and so the problem persists. Everyone sees it, but no one owns it. Why is this? Unless midwives *'act with honesty and integrity at all times, treating people fairly and without discrimination, bullying or harassment'* (NMC, 2018), we are breaching our regulatory code.

VALUE: bullying

Surely tackling an issue that causes staff *'anxiety and depression, disengagement and isolation, reduced confidence and impacts on home life'* (NHS Employers, 2022) should be a priority for all. This, alongside the association of bullying with *'greater risk of human error, poorer patient care, reduced productivity lower morale, increased absenteeism and reduced teamwork'* (NHS Employers, 2022), further endorses the need for action not discussion.

Professional midwifery advocates (PMAs) spend much of their time facilitating staff well-being and bullying is a concern. PMAs can support staff through the process of restorative clinical supervision (RCS). They can explore how poor behaviour can be addressed in facilitated discussion. The role of the PMA is not to 'fix' things or give advice but to provide time, space and supportive professional challenge where supervisees can seek their own solutions.

Alice: professional midwifery advocate

It is 07:30 and I have commenced my routine PMA walkaround. This is something I do at the beginning of all my shifts to check on the well-being of the staff about to commence and finish their shifts. I am approached by Drew, an experienced nurse and a qualified midwife of three years, who has just finished the night shift. Drew looks distressed and asks to see me.

EVIDENCE: RCS has been shown to have a positive impact on the well-being of staff (Pettit and Stephen, 2015)

I find a private space where we can talk. Drew is visibly shaken while recalling the events of the previous shift. For the past few months, a senior member of staff has been derogatory in their behaviour towards him. This behaviour has been witnessed by colleagues. It escalated during the night, causing Drew to question his value as a midwife as well as his worth as a human being. Drew reports feeling extremely low in mood and hurt that none of his colleagues sought to see if he was okay following the derogatory remarks and his apparent bullying.

Reflections

PMA reflection by Alice

My experience of Drew is that he is confident, engaged and vivacious. He always appears to have had positive relationships with his colleagues and with those he cares for and is, in my view, an excellent role model.

I was pleased that Drew wanted to talk. I recognised the scenario he described from my own experience and needed to remind myself that this was Drew's story. My role was to listen and give Drew a safe space to offload the way he was feeling to enable him to let go of the emotion, contain his thoughts and know that he had been heard.

VALUES: compassion, caring, communication

Drew said that the night had drained him and that he was 'feeling all over the place'. I asked him to share with me what 'feeling all over the place' meant to him. This offered Drew the opportunity to expand on something meaningful

THEORY: repeating the same words demonstrates active listening to him that I would otherwise have no frame of reference for. We sat in silence for a while. He went on to describe his feelings of loss of self-worth and that he was increasingly feeling that midwifery was no longer what he wanted to do. He didn't understand why he had allowed himself to be spoken to as he was or why he wasn't able to let it just wash over him as he had on previous occasions. He talked about how the night shifts exhausted him in a way that they never used to and that he was feeling at *'rock bottom'*. I asked whether he felt that there were any other aspects of life that were affecting the way that he felt about work. He could not think of anything but commented that the way he felt about work was putting a strain on his usually happy home life. I asked Drew what he meant by *'rock bottom'* and just how bad it felt to be there. Drew said that he *'was as low as he had ever been'*, and that he needed to talk to try to put things into perspective. As PMAs in our hospital Trust, we have a direct referral system to a clinical psychologist; I explored this option with Drew. He assured me that he would seek further help if he needed it or if he ever felt low enough to self-harm. Drew continued to talk about his feelings about midwifery. I asked: *'What is it that keeps you coming to work?'* He looked at me and rolled his eyes, saying *'the mortgage'* and gave a wry smile. He talked about the buzz that he still got from providing good care despite the constraints, the positive feedback from women and, generally, the camaraderie that he felt with his colleagues. He loved the feeling of being part of a good team. He reflected on the night and wondered if that lack of camaraderie, of the 'team', was part of his concern, the job being hard enough at times without unsupportive colleagues as well. I asked: *'What do you think could be done about this?'* He sighed and said: *'I know what I have to do. I have to address it; I just need to think about how.'* Drew was looking tired but calmer. The Drew I knew was mulling over his options. I recapped what I understood to be his concerns: that he had had a bad shift in which he had been spoken to harshly by a colleague who he felt had shown disrespect towards him in a publicly humiliating way. He had felt powerless to respond, possibly because it was not the first time that this had happened. Drew was

THEORY: silence can be calming and gives an opportunity for uninterrupted thought

EVIDENCE: the negative feelings that Drew identifies are associated with bullying and harassment (NHS Employers, 2022)

THEORY: powerful questions are open-ended and ask why? how? what? who? when? where? They encourage discussion and facilitate exploration

VALUES: respect, courage, communication

disappointed that he had not addressed the issue at the time, or previously; he recognised that this needed to be done as the situation could not be left to continue. He was also upset that none of his colleagues supported him. He still loved midwifery but did not like how this episode had made him feel. I asked if I had missed or misinterpreted anything or if he wanted to say anything else. Drew agreed that this was what he had talked about and added that he would think about his next steps. He thanked me for the opportunity to share the way that he was feeling. He said he felt less muddled and that he might sleep easier today. I asked if Drew would like to meet again when he had thought further about what he would like to do. He agreed to contact me next week.

VALUE: compassion

I was left in a dilemma, wondering if the co-ordinator also needed support. It is hard to understand why people misuse their power to belittle their colleagues, but she too may be stressed and this is how it is manifesting. She also may have been bullied and could see this behaviour as the norm. I cannot make any assumptions and I cannot address this directly as it could breach Drew's confidentiality. I could ask a PMA colleague to ensure to include her in a welfare check. If she lacks self-awareness though, she may just say that she is fine. PMAs report back themes but take care to maintain the privacy of the supervisee. I am wondering if this is an occasion where if harm is being caused to others, a more direct approach is needed. I really need Drew to do this.

Drew's reflections

On the drive home, I was thinking and realised that there was more to the situation than I had discussed with Alice. I used to love midwifery; it's my passion. Being able to support and empower women and their partners to experience the most positive experience possible, in one of the most important moments of their lives, is a privilege. Ever since I moved into midwifery from nursing, I have always felt like an impostor in a female-dominant workforce; as a student, the midwives would check with the women not that they were happy to have a student present but, notably, if they were happy to have a male student care for them. This has continued since qualifying and frequently I get mistaken by women, partners and new staff as a doctor, or I am known as the male midwife rather than Drew, a midwife (Pendleton, 2015). Before I would embrace this as a challenge, a chance to show that I am just as capable as any other midwife regardless of my gender. I would get lovely feedback from the women I cared for and from the students who worked with me and accepted me as the experienced healthcare professional I am. In the past few months this has all changed, and the culture where I work has become toxic. There are cliques of midwives who undermine and bully more junior staff to empower themselves, and favour their friends within the clique. They allocate women with additional care needs and complexities of co-morbidity to staff who may be less experienced and who they wish to intimidate. On many shifts, I have witnessed this group of midwives, who include multiple co-ordinators, laughing and sniggering at junior staff who are struggling with the additional complex care cases they have been assigned. They significantly belittle them if they call for help when the co-ordinator feels it is not appropriate. I should have stood up for these midwives, my colleagues, but if I did I thought I would be next; I would become a target (Darbyshire et al, 2019).

I realise now I became a target anyway by not being one of the bully's team players but the 'male midwife'; I stood out. It started three months ago with a woman I was caring for who had complex needs. When her baby was born, she was well with excellent Apgar scores. However, an hour after birth the baby began to struggle with respiratory effort and her condition deteriorated quickly. I got help and conducted the appropriate care. She was admitted to the neonatal intensive care unit, diagnosed later with a cardiac anomaly and referred to a specialist paediatric hospital. All of this was not pre-empted and was a shock to us all, especially the woman and her family. Gossip quickly spread throughout the maternity department about this case, and I heard whispering about it behind my back. I would hear

THEORY: unconscious bias. Unconscious bias impacts on every decision that we make in and outside of work. False assumptions of people can lead to negative outcomes and decisions that may lead to professional incompetence (Sporek, 2015). NHS England recommends all healthcare professionals complete cultural competence and unconscious bias training as part of the Maternity Transformation Programme to provide personalised care to women following the publication of the Better Births report (NHS England, 2016) staff members say: *'Yes, it was the male midwife looking after that baby'* and *'what was he thinking not getting help when the baby was born'* and *'can't believe there was no sign something was wrong on the cardiotocograph; he must have made a mistake. Wouldn't want him looking after me'*.

From then on, I have been spoken to like I no longer have experience, intellect or, more importantly, feelings. I feel the co-ordinator who worked last night is the instigator with her group of midwifery bullies. I don't know what to do. I'll sleep on it and arrange to meet with Alice next week.

Next meeting

Alice

MODEL: the RCS process

Drew and I met for a planned and structured meeting to further explore the issues that he had identified. We were in a private room where we would not be disturbed. We discussed the 'supervision contract'. This is considered good practice but is not always appropriate for ad hoc sessions when emotions are running high. We spoke about the aim of the RCS session and its goal. We reminded ourselves of the confidential nature of the exchange, and that all information would be kept between us unless there were any safeguarding issues or any risks to others revealed. If this were to be the case, I would support Drew to escalate the concern to the appropriate person. We agreed that the session would last for one hour and that notes would only be kept by Drew if he wanted to take them. Drew had brought some notes with him; he had clearly thought about the situation and prepared for the session.

MODEL: active listening

We 'checked in' to the session to focus on the process. Drew explored his thoughts. I reminded myself that I needed to listen, to understand rather than to contribute and to concentrate on what Drew was saying.

Drew told me that he had felt much better after our previous meeting. He had been ready to hand in his notice that day but thinking about the reasons he became a midwife had made him rethink this. I asked him to share with me what he thought his options were. He knew that he could approach his manager and follow the Human Resources (HR) policy with regard to dignity in the workplace. Also, he wondered if there was a gender issue: that he was being picked on because he was a man in a woman's world. Drew is a member of a trade union and confident that he would get support from his local steward but not from those colleagues who had witnessed the event. It would be *'his word against hers'*. He did not like the thought of what would happen to him once the supporters of the co-ordinator found out that he had reported her. He talked about the workplace 'cliques' and the way they create a toxic environment, where only those who are part of the group felt emotionally, and sometimes professionally, safe. I asked if he had considered talking to the Trust 'Speak Up Guardian' on the confidential helpline, but he did not feel that would be any more useful than the HR route. *'I need to address the behaviour with the person directly'*, he said. *'I can't let her get away with speaking to me in the way that she did; it isn't fair to me and if I don't say something, she'll think it's okay to do it to everyone. I don't know if it will make any difference, but I can't ignore it. I won't do it imme-diately. I need time to think it through. I get up in the morning not wanting to come to work; I feel disillusioned and com-pletely lacking in energy. I feel "burnt out".'* I acknowledged Drew's feelings and asked: *'Remind me, why are you still a midwife?'* He talked in positive terms of the satisfaction he got from doing his job well. *'How do you know that you do it well?'* I asked. He smiled as he told me of the positive feedback, the cards and 'thank-yous', and the delight that he felt when stopped in the street by grateful mothers and their partners. *'Midwifery can be such a fabulous job'*, he said. It was good to hear Drew identify those things him-self. It can be wearing to hear someone else talk positively about midwifery when you are not feeling it. False reassurances and energetic enthusiasm can lead to 'toxic positivity', where negative feelings are dismissed, causing further unhappiness.

> **VALUES:** bullying and harassment are behaviours that make someone feel intimidated or offended; they are often not differentiated. In United Kingdom law, bullying is not illegal; harassment is, if the harassment is related to a protected characteristic, sex in this instance, Drew would have grounds for a formal complaint (Equality Act 2010)

> **THEORY:** toxic positivity

Drew remarked: *'I don't feel that I can give my all when I feel as stressed as I do. Perhaps I have reached a point in my career where I need a change. I don't have the energy to take on a formal process to deal with the bullying. I'm going to look for another job.'* Drew had a plan.

I closed the session with a recap of our discussion. My understanding was that Drew had considered his options for dealing with the bullying and felt that the formal HR route via his manager or 'Speak Up Guardian' were not his preferred options. He felt exhausted, had no faith in the system and would prefer to address the issue directly with the co-ordinator when he felt able. Meanwhile, he would consider whether his future lay elsewhere. He recognised that he was not giving his best here as he felt stressed and 'burnt out'. Drew agreed that this was a fair summing up. He felt better for having some clarity and direction. I asked Drew if it would help to meet again to run through how he might approach his conversation with the co-ordinator in a 'practice rehearsal'. He said that he felt it would be useful. We checked out of the session.

I reported the themes of bullying, disrespect and potential attrition in my monthly PMA activities return. I also logged a concern with regard to cliques in the workplace. These themes are reported to our management team via our governance committee. It concerns me that our 'caring profession' cares so little for its own. And that bullying is happening in my Trust. Our PMA team are redoubling our efforts to act. We are taking ownership of this. We will improve our workplace culture. We have potential solutions; we must make them work.

Drew

I was so glad I had arranged a meeting with Alice; she always listens to what I have to say, and I always feel valued. She does not advise me but helps me talk through the emotions I am feeling, allowing me to explore all the dilemmas I am facing, and in turn the actions I could take.

THEORY: restorative clinical supervision

Through the RCS session with Alice, I realised how much my love for midwifery has been affected. I no longer enjoy coming to work and the impact is having a huge detrimental effect on my personal life. Alice asked me to think about the potential options I have to move forward. I feel very strongly that my dignity has been truly destroyed by these midwives; however, what can one person do to stop it? Even if I speak to my manager or go to Human Resources with my union representative, will this stop the toxic environment the department has become? I keep thinking is it possible? Can one person bring about this much change? In my heart I know that the reality is that even if the co-ordinator was spoken to, the rest of the clique will continue and if they know it was me that reported her, then I will become an even bigger target than I am now. My career will be over.

VALUE: bullying

My other option and the one I am going to take is to look for jobs elsewhere; find somewhere where I will be valued. My passion for midwifery is still there and during my discussion with Alice I realised I am not ready for someone else to decide my career is over. I have decided as soon as I get home from work today, I am applying for new jobs at different trusts, trusts where there is potential for growth and professional development. I am going to speak to my GP and ask for some time off sick for mental well-being; I cannot keep going in on shift anxious and stressed, with limited sleep from all the worrying. It doesn't feel comfortable not taking action to stop the bullying and victimisation. I asked Alice for her thoughts and she told me about Speak Up Guardians. I wondered maybe when I resign, I could speak to them and tell them the truth without having the repercussions from the bullies attacking me. I know they say it's confidential, but is it? When people bully specific individuals? I think if I resign, I could stand up and say something, as what can they do to me then? And I will feel better for addressing the issue rather than ignoring it.

VALUES: self-care, compassion, caring

I am scared and feel sad to leave what I thought a few years ago was a work family, but I guess people change, staff change and now it's my turn to move forward and not look back.

Questions for reflection and discussion

1. How might you have supported Drew as a concerned colleague?

2. Have you ever felt like Drew? What did you do about it?

3. Have you ever witnessed bullying in your workplace? If so, what did you do about it?

4. What recommendations could you make to promote a healthy culture within your maternity department?

5. Have you accessed any of the toolkits to promote civility in the workplace? (See helpful resources.)

6. What are your personal actions for quality improvement around bullying and harassment in your workplace?

Helpful resources

NHS Employers (2019) *Professionalism and Cultural Transformation (PACT) Toolkit* – www.nhsemployers.org/publications/professionalism-and-cultural-transformation-pact-toolkit

NHS England and NHS Improvement (2020) *NHSi Civility and Respect Toolkit* – www.socialpartnershipforum.org/system/files/2021-10/Shortened-Version-NHSEI%20-Civility-Respect-Toolkit.pdf

Psychology Today (2023) Toxic Positivity – www.psychologytoday.com/gb/basics/toxic-positivity

Royal College of Obstetricians & Gynaecologists (nd) *Workplace Behaviour Toolkit* – www.rcog.org.uk/careers-and-training/starting-your-og-career/workforce/improving-workplace-behaviours/workplace-behaviour-toolkit

References

ACAS (2021) Handling a Bullying, Harassment or Discrimination Complaint at Work. [online] Available at: www.acas.org.uk/handling-a-bullying-harassment-discrimination-complaint (accessed 19 December 2022).

Bharj, K and Marshall, J (2019) Becoming a Midwife: The History and Socialization into Professional Practice. In Marshall, J E (ed) *Myles Professional Studies for Midwifery Education and Practice: Concepts and Challenges* (pp 1–18). Cambridge, MA: Elsevier.

Darbyshire, P, Thompson D and Watson R (2019) Nursing's Future? Eat Young, Spit Out, Repeat. Endlessly. *Journal of Nursing Management*, 27(7): 1337–40.

Equality Act (2010). [online] Available at: www.legislation.gov.uk/ukpga/2010/15/contents (accessed 14 April 2023).

NHS England (2016) *National Maternity Review. Better Births: Improving Outcomes of Maternity Services in England – A Five Year Forward View for Maternity Care.* [online] Available at: www.engl and.nhs.uk/wp-content/uploads/2016/02/national-maternity-review-report.pdf (accessed 19 December 2022).

NHS Employers (2022) Tackling Bullying in the NHS Infographic. [online] Available at: www. nhsemployers.org/articles/tackling-bullying-nhs-infographic (accessed 9 March 2023).

Nursing & Midwifery Council (NMC) (2018) *The Code: Professional Standards of Practice and Behaviour for Nurses, Midwives and Nursing Associates.* London: Nursing & Midwifery Council.

Pendleton, J (2015) What's It Like Being a Male Midwife? *British Journal of Midwifery*, 23(7): 466–8.

Pettit, A and Stephen, R (2015) *Supporting Health Visitors and Fostering Resilience.* London: Institute of Health Visiting.

Sporek, P (2015) Unconscious Bias. *British Journal of Midwifery*, 23(12).

Case study 13
Andrea: not my day

Georgina Sosa and Jemma Thorne

Introduction

This case study describes decisions of a community midwife who is transferring Andrea in labour from home where she has been receiving one-to-one care to an obstetric-led maternity unit where the care may be provided by more than one professional (one-to-many). It focuses on the decision to move including shared decision making with Andrea and her partner, Mattia, framing the decision so both are empowered and enabled to feel supported (resilience building). The professional concerns of the midwife about the reception they may receive from their peers on the unit (territorialism) are explored.

Labouring at home

I arrived at Andrea's flat on a Monday at 12:36 to support her for a homebirth. I could see the relief and happiness in Mattia's (Andrea's partner) eyes when the front door opened. Mattia guided me to a space prepared for my labour and birth equipment. The relationship was familiar as I had cared for Andrea in her pregnancy, and I communicated with her over the weekend when she was experiencing irregular contractions. Assessing Andrea, who was nulliparous, in labour, I noted that she was contracting regularly. In between the contractions I gained a history, and I watched Andrea pacing the living room. She stopped when she felt the contractions start and focused on breathing with her eyes closed, zoned in to her body's sensations. Intermittently, Mattia whispered in her ear and touched her hands tenderly. There was an ease shared between them that was noticeable when Andrea dropped her shoulders and relaxed in between the contractions as she prepared herself to pace the room once more. I also noted that Andrea was instinctively placing one leg up on the sofa and rotating her hips and described feeling discomfort in her back. I recognised these markers as signs

MODEL: physiological birth

EVIDENCE: upright positions and movement in labour reduces the length of labour and caesarean section (Lawrence et al, 2013)

VALUE: the Code (NMC, 2018)

VALUE: shared decision making

THEORY: support for birthing partners. Partners can feel 'powerless and useless' and need time to 'recharge their batteries' in the labour situation (Tarlazzi et al, 2015, pp 190, 192)

MODEL: home birth, birthplace study (Hollowell, 2011)

that the fetus may be in the occipitoposterior position. I asked for consent to perform maternal observations, which were all within normal limits, and an examination. I palpated Andrea's abdomen on the sofa. I felt a right occipitoposterior position, the head three-fifths palpable. I did not perform a vaginal examination initially as Andrea and I agreed it was obvious that she was in labour. Contractions were regular, every three minutes, strong, lasting 50 seconds. I encouraged Andrea to listen to her body.

Mattia was inflating the birthing pool between the contractions. He did not have the opportunity to do a practice run. I could hear some cursing words coming from the bedroom, maybe an indication that Mattia was feeling nervous. I recalled Andrea really wanting a homebirth, while Mattia was not so keen but wanted to support Andrea's choice. I asked Mattia if I could help, and my presence was welcomed. I helped Mattia empty all the equipment from their borrowed birthing pool box, and we started to set the pool up in the living room. We found a rhythm between Andrea pacing and then breathing through the contractions, with Mattia intermittently providing emotional support and me completing the observations. This also included auscultating the baby's heart rate immediately after a contraction every 15 minutes in a position Andrea wished to adopt, in line with National Institute for Health and Care Excellence guidance for monitoring in labour (NICE, 2022).

I spotted a packet of opened sugary sweets on a table, and a shower curtain to protect the furnishings on a beanbag, two of the many recommendations discussed at the 36-week home visit, as part of the tick list to facilitate a home birth. I remembered so vividly the conversation about the pros and cons regarding the places of birth. We also discussed different scenarios which may prevent the facilitation of a homebirth, including transfer to hospital in labour if needed.

The first time I listened to Andrea's preferences for a homebirth was at her booking interview when she was at eight weeks' gestation. Throughout Andrea's pregnancy we developed an excellent rapport; we had a mutual respect for the expertise we both held. Knowing Andrea throughout the pregnancy helped me when assessing how Andrea was coping in her labour.

MODEL: continuity of carer

Ninety minutes after my arrival, Andrea requested a vaginal examination and took me to her bedroom. I repeated the abdominal palpation which showed no change. I then performed a vaginal examination, which showed the cervix to be in the mid position, softening, 5 cm dilated, membranes felt, and one oblique suture was identified which supported the right occipitoposterior position. When I went back into the living room, Mattia had finished inflating the pool and was now being challenged by connecting the hose to a tap to get it filling. Between us and with some humour, we started to fill the pool.

VALUE: shared decision making

Shortly afterwards, Andrea came into the living room with a smile on her face when she saw the inflated birthing pool. Keen to get in, she stripped down to a bikini and gently lowered herself in, with instant relief from the water. As the hours passed, Andrea appeared to be advancing in labour and asked for some Entonox. I set up the cylinder by the pool and demonstrated how to use it. Mattia continued to provide the emotional support and I was providing increasingly more reassurance and encouragement with the contractions.

Four hours had passed since the last vaginal examination (VE) and Andrea was keen to know how she was progressing. NICE advises to offer a VE every four hours or if there is concern about progress or in response to a woman's wishes. The vaginal examination findings showed no change and I explained this gently to Andrea and Mattia. With disappointment on their faces, I gave them reassurance and explored other ways to help progress labour. Andrea shared how the back pain was very intense and she was feeling vulnerable and tired and growing more concerned about the occipitoposterior position. Within the hour, Andrea made the decision to transfer to hospital as she was tired and wanted more analgesia.

EVIDENCE: intrapartum care for healthy women and babies (NICE, 2017)

VALUE: shared decision making

VALUES: professional responsibility, safety

EVIDENCE: Sosa et al (2018a)

VALUE: informed choice. In cases of intrapartum transfer, women are known to experience a sense of abandonment when their midwife is unable to stay with them (Kuliukas et al, 2016)

THEORY: territorial behaviour manifests itself as a feeling of 'us versus them' behaviours, feeling under scrutiny and being aware of conflicting ideologies (Sosa et al, 2018a)

I telephoned the delivery suite co-ordinator to inform them that Andrea was transferring to the labour ward. I then arranged for an ambulance transfer into the hospital. There was never any question I would do this immediately, but my mind started to question what the hospital staff would think of me. I started to review my one-to-one support in labour through the hospital medicalised lens. I felt quite emotional, but I managed to keep my voice strong on the telephone. I did not want to cause Andrea and Mattia more anxiety. I knew that transfer from home to hospital is a stressful experience for those in labour and their birthing partner/s. My priority was to focus on the needs of Andrea and organise the ambulance. I contemplated for a minute whether I should ask Mattia to drive Andrea to the hospital with me following closely behind. My mind was constantly questioning whether I was making the right choices, but I knew it was my place to stay with Andrea and Mattia. During this contemplation, I continued the labour observations. Andrea's contractions had slowed down. I knew this was likely to be linked to the anxiety about the transfer affecting her oxytocin levels. I made time while waiting for the ambulance to prepare and manage Andrea and Mattia's expectations of the transfer and hospital care.

The paramedics arrived and looked to me for my clinical expertise, a mutual respect for each other's professions. Andrea lived on the first floor and insisted on walking down the stairs to the ambulance. I helped Andrea into the ambulance and she was strapped to the ambulance trolley; Mattia followed the ambulance by car. I empathised with Andrea; she was unable to mobilise in the ambulance and I knew this would increase her pain and anxiety. I felt a responsibility that I was the link between the one-to-one care at home and the hospital care. I had to provide emotional support for Andrea to make that transition.

At the same time, I also became more anxious about the hospital staff scrutinising my labour care. I started to reflect, rechecking if my care was appropriate and timely. I did not want the hospital staff to think I was lazy or incompetent. As we got closer to the hospital, I knew I was likely to be met with territorial behaviour. The delivery suite staff all looked my way when we entered the delivery suite. Seeing a labouring woman enter on a paramedic's trolley always causes everybody to look up. I felt scrutinised before I had stepped into a room. I was guided to Room 2 and told a midwife would follow shortly to take over the care.

I helped Andrea onto the bed while two midwives brought equipment into the room. One midwife was the delivery suite co-ordinator and the other was taking over Andrea's care. I provided a history of my care using the SBAR tool. I encouraged Andrea and Mattia to contribute to the hand-over discussion. I observed the anxiety in Andrea and Mattia's eyes as they scanned the labour room, looking at the equipment around them. I quickly provided explanations about the items: an electronic fetal monitor, a cannula, automated blood pressure machine, a trolley with the epidural equipment and a neonatal resuscitaire. I knew that Andrea's care would be medicalised from this point on. An obstetrician, anaesthetist and anaesthetic assistant entered the room, introduced themselves and started discussing the assessment to be completed and the epidural procedure. When health professionals introduce themselves, it helps the mental transition from one-to-one to one-to-many carers (Sosa et al, 2018a), but I was conscious there were six health professionals in the labour room. I suddenly became aware that the care had transferred from one-to-one to one-to-many. I saw Andrea look around at all the faces and she gave me a look that communicated she was not ready for this. I took Andrea's hand and asked if she wanted five minutes with Mattia to adjust to these new surroundings. The professionals hearing her say yes then left the room. I heard a comment from the two midwives noting that Andrea had not been cannulated yet, inferring I should have done so before this point. I hoped that Andrea and Mattia did not hear this comment as I did not want them to lose their trust in me. As much as I wanted to be the main caregiver for Andrea, I recognised that the time was coming to relinquish the role and hand over the care to the hospital midwives. I said my goodbyes and left.

THEORY: transfer of care. Transition time is needed to adjust from a one-to-one to one-to-many environment (Sosa et al, 2018a)

Reflections

I felt disappointed when on abdominal palpation I had identified the baby lying in the occipitoposterior position. There is not a great deal of research around this malposition but I had discussed with Andrea and Mattia at the 36-week visit that persistent occipitoposterior position can prolong labour. Rather than discussing these points again in the labour, I encouraged Andrea's intuitive movements and to listen to her body and remain active. The home environment is more conducive for such intuitive behaviours. Most women labour well when they remain in their own environment, in positions they have chosen (Chapman, 2017).

EVIDENCE: the occipitoposterior position is the most common malposition and the labour is likely to be slower and more painful, so women need a great deal of support and positive encouragement. There is an increased likelihood of caesarean section or perineal trauma (Chapman, 2017; Tempest et al, 2019; Moura et al, 2022). However, persistent occipitoposterior position is estimated at 1.8–12.9 per cent so there was a high chance that the fetus would rotate to occipito anterior position (Moura et al, 2022)

Another focus of reflection concerned my resilience. From the moment the decision was made for Andrea to transfer to hospital, I started doubting all my clinical judgements. Could I have done more to help this baby change position at home? How should we transfer into hospital? Will the hospital staff feel I am incompetent? These thoughts took my focus away from Andrea and Mattia. Reflecting on attributes of resilience, I could have contacted a trusted midwifery colleague to reflect on my care and possible actions before speaking to the delivery suite staff about transferring Andrea to the hospital. I should have possessed self-belief in the one-to-one care I provided and the clinical decisions I made. I successfully supported the choices of Andrea and Mattia and the transfer was completed under safe conditions. In addition, continuity was achieved until the handover of care at the hospital, which has been shown to help with the transition from one-to-one care at home to one-to-many at the hospital. Overall, I should have been optimistic about the transfer to hospital. It is part of the continuum of maternity care so transfer should not be viewed as a failure. Such optimism may have been achieved if I reviewed my one-to-one support through the lens of midwifery-led care rather than through a medicalised lens.

MODEL: building resilience (Clohessy et al, 2019)

THEORY: midwifery-led care in labour. Sosa et al (2018b) identified six themes that midwives balance when caring for a labouring person within midwife-led birth environments

Actions

In future I will give more thought to how to frame the discussion about the transfer to the delivery suite. Rather than viewing the birth plan as a tick list, I will include choices available, research evidence, benefits and risks and check the knowledge, values and beliefs of the childbearing person. In the NICE (2017) intrapartum guidelines, there is a section concerning transfer to the delivery suite that includes discussing choices available, research evidence, benefits and risks but also incorporates practical items needed for transfer including clothing to wear and mode of transport available for the birthing partner. I will also add another point: how I, the midwife, can support the transition from the home to the hospital setting. Documenting this shared decision making has the potential to reduce anxieties for all concerned during labour/post-partum transfers to the delivery suite.

MODEL: shared decision making (NICE, 2021)

Actions I will aim to repeat in the future include enhancing the physiological processes while recognising risk factors for transfer and acting early as it is important. I will continue to provide one-to-one support for as long as possible when arriving on the delivery suite. If I have the option of continuing the care on the delivery suite until my shift change, I will do it, as this has been shown to increase the resilience of people in labour.

EVIDENCE: the recent Ockenden report highlighted how midwives 'can become so focussed on achieving a physiological birth' that women and their babies can be placed in harm (Ockenden, 2022)

EVIDENCE: Sosa et al (2018a)

Questions for reflection and discussion

1. In what ways do you feel anxious about your care being scrutinised by the maternity staff when transferring a labouring person from the home to the delivery suite? Does this fear affect your decision making?

2. What actions do you think could eradicate the 'us versus them' territorial working culture to encourage collaborative and respectful working relationships?

3. Explore the model of community midwifery within your organisation and the opportunities for continuity of care.

4. Reflect on the use of a shared decision-making tool when documenting your discussions and decisions in pregnancy about potential transfers to the delivery suite in labour or post-partum.

5. How would you view your resilience in the workplace when considering your self-belief, optimism and how you network with colleagues to gain affirmation and support? Do you need to work on your resilience?

6. If you had the choice, would you have stayed in the delivery suite with Andrea until the end of your shift? Can you think of other interventions that could have helped Andrea and Mattia with their transition from one-to-one support at home to one-to-many in the hospital setting?

Helpful resource

Reflecting on Resilience in Midwifery – www.all4maternity.com/reflecting-resilience-midwifery

References

Chapman, V (2017) *The Midwife's Labour and Birth Handbook*. 4th ed. Oxford: Wiley Blackwell.

Clohessy, N, McKellar, L and Fleet, J (2019) Understanding Resilience in the Context of Midwifery: A Concept Analysis. *Evidence Based Midwifery*, 17(1): 10–18.

Hollowell, J (2011) Birthplace Programme Overview: Background, Component Studies and Summary of Findings. *Birthplace in England Research Programme. Final Report Part 1*. NIHR Service Delivery and Organisation programme. [online] Available at: www.npeu.ox.ac.uk/assets/downloads/birthplace/Birthplace_Report_1_-_Programme_overview.pdf (accessed 9 March 2023).

Kuliukas, L, Lewis, L, Hauck, Y L and Duggan, R (2016) Midwives' Experience of Transfer in Labour from a Western Australian Birth Centre Co-located to a Tertiary Maternity Hospital. *Women and Birth*, 29: 18–23.

Lawrence, A, Lewis, L, Hofmeyr, G J and Styles, C (2013) Maternal Positions and Mobility During First Stage Labour. *Cochrane Database of Systematic Reviews*, 2013, Issue 8: Art. No. CD003934. [online] Available at: www.cochranelibrary.com/cdsr/doi/10.1002/14651858.CD003934.pub3/full (accessed 22 December 2022).

Moura, R, Borges, M, Oliveira, D, Parente, M, Kimmich, N and Mascarenhas, T (2022) A Biomechanical Study of the Birth Position: A Natural Struggle between Mother and Fetus. *Biomechanics and Modeling in Mechanobiology*, 21: 937–51. [online] Available at: https://link.springer.com/article/10.1007/s10237-022-01569-2 (accessed 22 December 2022).

National Institute for Health and Care Excellence (NICE) (2017) *Intrapartum Care for Healthy Women and Babies*. CG 190. London. NICE.

National Institute for Health and Care Excellence (NICE) (2021) Shared Decision Making. NG197. [online] Available at: www.nice.org.uk/about/what-we-do/our-programmes/nice-guidance/nice-guidelines/shared-decision-making (accessed 9 March 2023).

National Institute for Health and Care Excellence (NICE) (2022) Fetal Monitoring in Labour. NG229. [online] Available at: www.nice.org.uk/guidance/ng229 (accessed 9 March 2023).

Nursing & Midwifery Council (NMC) (2018) *The Code: Professional Standards of Practice and Behaviour for Nurses, Midwives and Nursing Associates*. London: Nursing & Midwifery Council.

Ockenden, D (2022) *Findings, Conclusions and Essential Actions from the Independent Review of Maternity Services at The Shrewsbury and Telford Hospital NHS Trust*. London: HMSO.

Sosa, G, Crozier, K and Stockl, A (2018a) The Experiences of Midwives and Women during Intrapartum Transfer from One-to-One Midwife-led Birthing Environments to Obstetric-led Units. *Midwifery*, 65: 43–50.

Sosa, G, Crozier, K and Stockl, A (2018b) Midwifery One-to-One Support in Labour: More Than a Ratio. *Midwifery*, 62: 230–9.

Tarlazzi, E, Chiari, P, Naldi, E, Parma, D and Jack, S M (2015) Italian Fathers' Experiences of Labour Pain. *British Journal of Midwifery*, 23(3): 188–94.

Tempest, N, Lane, S and Hapangama, D (2019) Babies in Occiput Posterior Position Are Significantly More Likely to Require an Emergency Cesarean Birth Compared with Babies in Occiput Transverse Position in the Second Stage of Labor: A Prospective Observational Study. *Acta Obstetricia et Gynecologica Scandinavica*, 99: 537–45. [online] Available at: https://obgyn.onlinelibrary.wiley.com/doi/10.1111/aogs.13765 (accessed 22 December 2022).

Conclusion

Kenda Crozier and Julia Hubbard

The clinical scenarios in this book have presented some of the decisions and dilemmas that midwives encounter in everyday practice in the UK. There are some key essential elements that are shared across the book in the values, theories and models; for example, person-centred care, safeguarding and communication are central to most of the clinical interactions you will have read about in this book. In each case, the actions of the midwife are underpinned by the Code (NMC, 2018), which outlines the expected professional conduct of nurses, midwives and nursing associates in the UK and the standards of proficiency for midwives (NMC, 2019). In addition the '6Cs' of care, compassion, competence, communication, courage and commitment (NHS England, 2017) have also been demonstrated across the midwives' interactions.

In some instances where there is no clear guideline or evidence to support decision making, midwives need to draw on their own values; the values of the profession, their professional knowledge and evidence that can be applied from elsewhere. An example of this is in the case of Oli, Case study 10, which illustrates that the maternity service has not yet adopted the inclusive language needed to meet his needs. The midwife is faced with the situation where the needs of the system (documentation) and needs of the client (a trans man) are not entirely compatible. Straddling this uncomfortable space is the midwife trying to educate themself and their colleagues without causing offence to the person at the centre of the care. The ethos of shared decision making is important to ensure that midwives work collaboratively with their clients and other professionals, and this process of sharing information to enable informed decisions to be taken jointly is illustrated across the book. Many of the case studies refer to recent reports in the UK where failings in care delivery and especially in decision making have been brought to light. By using evidence to underpin their decisions, midwives can ensure that care is delivered according to the highest-quality available knowledge. By providing clients with the best available evidence and having discussions that include options and choices, decisions can be taken in a shared and transparent way, taking account of the clients' wishes and beliefs. The belief systems of the client are not always in agreement with the medical evidence and this too can create an uncomfortable space in which to work. The case of Samia, Case study 1, illustrates this, where we encounter an educated person, very able to make autonomous decisions but who is not convinced by the advice of the medical experts, preferring to use her own belief system to support decisions about her health and that of her baby. The cultural belief systems highlighted in the case of Sara, Case study 8, demonstrate how safeguarding and law must come before the wishes of a client and their partner. The midwife in Sara's case was clear about their duty in law to protect Sara and also to safeguard the baby against the possibility of FGM by explaining the legal position.

We also see the difficulty placed on midwives by restrictions in the health system. Covid-19 created a new set of challenges through the way in which infection control systems created barriers to the usual ways of working. For example, the restrictions on partners attending hospital appointments and the potential communication barriers created by wearing personal protective equipment is demonstrated in the case of Lucy, Case study 11. Unlike some areas of healthcare which could be conducted remotely or put on pause, the safe conduct of facilitating birth needed to be carried out in the usual way with added infection control precautions. This meant that partners who are usually so integral to the support process were not able to access birthing units unless labour was established. We also see the difficulties of staffing levels and decisions and dilemmas created in trying to balance the needs of individuals and the needs of a system in which midwives work. Although Covid-19 is now considered to be endemic, the case study brings to light the way that changes can be implemented quickly and later adapted to support service users. This is contrary to the more considered approach to change that involves co-production and shared decisions to enhance services to meet the needs of clients.

The working relationships in many of the case studies highlight the value of coaching models (Molly and Sandra, Case study 5), models of resilience (Andrea, Case study 13) and restorative supervision (Drew, Case study 12). The confidence to challenge the decisions of other professionals is necessary in the autonomous practice of midwives, yet resilience and psychological safety issues are real and require attention in order to ensure that there is a safe system of care for all.

Professional development is required to practise safely, draw on up-to-date evidence and use models that are new or adapted from other areas. The UK health system is under strain and numerous reports have found that communication within the system and a failure to listen to the needs of those using its maternity services has resulted in poor care and outcomes for women and babies. A number of case studies highlight the territorialism and issues of communication between different areas of maternity care. The examples of territorial behaviour between professionals in midwifery-led birthing units and the delivery suite, as well as the nervousness shown by a midwife transferring care from the community to hospital, shows there are concerns about psychological safety in referrals. The confidence in decision making shown in the clear process of differential diagnosis and referral illustrates best practice in midwifery in the cases of baby Alex, Case study 4, and Amira, Case study 7. Developing the confidence and building the resilience to have the professional conversations that ensure shared decision making is fundamental to your own professional development but also to the safe care you provide. The support of a professional midwifery advocate, as in the case of Drew, can enable you to reflect on your practice and to enable you to build your knowledge and confidence.

Table C1 on the following pages provides an overall picture of the key theories, values and models in the book. The case studies of course contain important evidence on which midwives draw currently. The evidence presented is usually case study specific and draws on a range of empirical research, guidelines and reports from confidential enquiries.

We hope that you have found this book useful for your professional development and that it aids you to reflect on your own decision making in practice.

References

NHS England (2017) *Introducing the 6Cs*. [online] Available at: www.england.nhs.uk/6cs/wp-content/uploads/sites/25/2015/03/introducing-the-6cs.pdf (accessed 5 January 2023).

Nursing & Midwifery Council (NMC) (2018) *The Code: Professional Standards of Practice and Behaviour for Nurses, Midwives and Nursing Associates*. London: Nursing & Midwifery Council.

Nursing & Midwifery Council (NMC) (2019) *Standards of Proficiency for Midwives*. [online] Available at: www.nmc.org.uk/globalassets/sitedocuments/standards/standards-of-proficiency-for-midwives.pdf (accessed 23 January 2023)

Case study	Theories	Values	Models	Evidence
1. Samia	cultural safety	autonomy, unconscious bias	informed consent	*The Black Maternity Experiences* report (2022) Birthrights UK's *Systemic Racism, Not Broken Bodies* (2022) *Maternity Experiences of Muslim Women from Racialised Minority Communities* (2022) NICE guidance
2. Imogen	safeguarding, territorial behaviour	care, commitment, empathy	informed consent, multi-professional working, public health	Royal College of Obstetricians and Gynaecologists (RCOG) (2017) Management of Breech Presentation
3. Martha	trauma-informed care	safeguarding, empathy	person-centred care, consent and capacity	*Saving Lives, Improving Mothers' Care – Lessons Learned to Inform Maternity Care from the UK and Ireland Confidential Enquiries into Maternal Deaths and Morbidity 2017–19.*
4. Baby Alex	evidence-based practice, novice to expert	courage, confidence	multi-professional working, professional boundaries	RCOG Green-top Guideline 68 NHS standards for NIPE
5. Molly and Sandra	coaching, novice to expert	safety, compassion	NMC Standards for Student Supervision and Assessment, communication and learner feedback	NICE CG190 RCOG Green-top Guideline 52
6. Katarzyna	hierarchy of decisions	autonomy, advocacy	staffing, birth choices	Birthplace England Study Ockenden report

7. Amira	person-centred care	professional referral	red flags, diagnostic frameworks, RCM Stepping up to Public Health model	Royal College of Physicians Toolkit 15, *Saving Lives, Improving Mothers' Care Core Report 2018–2020*
8. Sara	safeguarding,	cultural norms, courage	legal frameworks, typology of FGM	WHO (2018b) RCOG Green-top Guideline 53
9. Rahaf	asylum seeking, social capital building	care, compassion, human rights	communication models, interpreting	NICE CG110 Research on the experiences of asylum seekers in the UK
10. Oli	gender identity, marginalisation, institutional erasure	communication, respect	person-centred care, inclusion, European Convention on Human Rights, Equality Act 2010	NICE CG192 Research on experiences of trans and non-binary parents
11. Lucy	risk assessment	communication, caring, compassion	evidence-based care, public health	RCOG Green-top Guideline 57
12. Drew	bullying, unconscious bias	advocacy, respect	restorative supervision, Equality Act 2010	restorative supervision
13. Andrea	territorialism, physiological birth	confidence, resilience	shared decision making	birthplace study, Hollowell (2011)

Table C1 Summary of key theories, values and models by case study

Index